Basic Behaviour Therapy

Douglas Murdoch

PhD
Lecturer in Psychiatry,
University of Calgary;
Clinical Psychologist, Alberta Children's Hospital

and

Philip Barker

MB, BS, FRCPsych, FRCP(C)
Professor of Psychiatry and Paediatrics,
University of Calgary;
Psychiatrist, Alberta Children's Hospital

OXFORD
BLACKWELL SCIENTIFIC PUBLICATIONS
LONDON EDINBURGH BOSTON
MELBOURNE PARIS BERLIN VIENNA

To Ann and Nathan – for your love, patience and for teaching
me more than any textbook could.

To Thembi, Sibusiso, Edmund, Lorna and Alice.

© 1991 by Douglas Murdoch & Philip Barker

Blackwell Scientific Publications
Editorial offices:
Osney Mead, Oxford OX2 0EL
25 John Street, London WC1N 2BL
23 Ainslie Place, Edinburgh EH3 6AJ
3 Cambridge Center, Cambridge,
  Massachusetts 02142, USA
54 University Street, Carlton,
  Victoria 3053, Australia

Other Editorial Offices:
Arnette SA
2, rue Casimir-Delavigne
75006 Paris
France

Blackwell Wissenschaft
Meinekestrasse 4
D-1000 Berlin 15
Germany

Blackwell MZV
Feldgasse 13
A-1238 Wien
Austria

First published 1991

Set by Excel Typesetters Co. Ltd.
Printed and bound in Great Britain by
Hartnolls Ltd, Bodmin, Cornwall

DISTRIBUTORS
Marston Book Services Ltd
PO Box 87
Oxford OX2 0DT
(*Orders*: Tel: 0865 791155
        Fax: 0865 791927
        Telex: 837515)

USA
Mosby-Year Book, Inc.
11830 Westline Industrial Drive
St Louis, Missouri 63146
(*Orders*: Tel: 800 633-6699)

Canada
Mosby-Year Book, Inc.
5240 Finch Avenue East
Scarborough, Ontario
(*Orders*: Tel: 416 298-1588)

Australia
Blackwell Scientific Publications
(Australia) Pty Ltd
54 University Street,
Carlton, Victoria 3053
(*Orders*: Tel: 03 347-0300)

British Library
Cataloguing in Publication Data
Murdoch, Douglas
  Basic behaviour therapy.
  1. Medicine. Behaviour therapy
  I. Title   II. Barker, Philip J.
  616.89142

ISBN 0-632-02322-8

Basic Behaviour Therapy

Also from Blackwell Scientific Publications

Basic Child Psychiatry
Fifth edition
Philip Barker
0-632-02063-6 (HB)
0-632-01923-9 (PB)

Basic Family Therapy
Second edition
Philip Barker
0-632-02228-0

Relapse Prevention for Addictive Behaviours
A Manual for Therapists
Shamil Wanigaratne, Wendy Wallace, Jane Pullin,
Francis Keaney, and Roger Farmer
0-632-02484-4

Basic Forensic Psychiatry
Malcolm Faulk
0-632-01926-3

Therapy with Couples
A Behavioural-Systems Approach to Marital
and Sexual Problems
Michael Crowe and Jane Ridley
0-632-2375-9

Counselling in HIV Infection and AIDS
Edited by John Green and Alana McCreaner
0-632-01924-7

HIV and AIDS in Mothers and Babies
Lorraine Sherr
0-632-02834-3

Counselling Drug Users about HIV and AIDS
Geraldine Mulleady
0-632-02939-0

Sex Therapy Manual
Patricia Gillan
0-632-01866-6

Contents

Foreword

Professor P.J. Graham, FRCP, FRCPsych, Professor of Child Psychiatry, Institute of Child Health, London

The last 30 years have seen remarkable developments in the use of behavioural techniques in treating psychological problems. In the 1950s, Hans Eysenck announced a new age when psychological therapies would be as scientifically based as those used for physical illnesses. Wolpe, Lazarus, Rachman and others published work in the late 1950s and early 1960s supporting this claim. Since then progress has been rapid.

It is therefore very appropriate that the existing textbooks on child psychiatry and family therapy by Philip Barker, already well established in the field, should now be complemented by a text in behaviour therapy. Mental health professionals, whether they be social workers, psychologists or psychiatrists, often complain that they do not find sufficient guidance on treatment even in the large, multi-author textbooks that are available. They need, and will find here in relation to behaviour therapy, a more extended discussion of therapeutic practice in the different modalities.

It is difficult for authors writing about therapy to achieve a balance, on the one hand between cookbook prescriptions which are likely to be inapplicable to most clients they see and, on the other, vague generalities that provide no practical assistance at all. However Douglas Murdoch and Philip Barker have succeeded in walking this tightrope in surefooted fashion, and, in my view, the book is neither too prescriptive, nor too vague.

One of the attractive features of the book is the emphasis given to the newer cognitive forms of behavioural treatments with which many readers will be unfamiliar. The Confucian saying 'Learning without thought is labour lost: thought without learning is perilous' is arguable, for certainly some permanent learning does occur without our thinking about it. But the recent acceptance of the importance of cognitive processes by behaviour therapists has not only widened the applicability of behavioural techniques, but has broadened their appeal both to professionals and to clients.

Of course, as the authors of this splendid book acknowledge, behavioural techniques are not a panacea. In some circumstances their use is inappropriate and in others their effects are modest.

Often their effectiveness is enhanced if they are combined with other approaches. But they do have increasingly wide application, and training in their use need not be as intense or time-consuming as in other forms of therapy. Further, though behaviour therapists recognise the need for great sensitivity and empathy in their work, many see it as an advantage that training in this form of treatment does not involve the same degree of self-exposure and soul-searching as is required with other approaches.

I am sure that mental health professionals, even those whose main orientation is psychodynamic, will find this an extremely useful account, easy to read and helpful in their practice.

Introduction

Basic Behaviour Therapy is designed for the newcomer to the field. It assumes no prior formal knowledge of the behavioural approach to solving or ameliorating human problems. Yet every one of us knows something – even if only intuitively – of learning theory and of how our responses may modify the behaviour of others. We know that people are apt to respond to rewards and encouragement, and also to certain forms of punishment. We know, too, that our everyday attempts to modify the behaviour of others are not always successful.

Behaviour therapy has developed from the study of how individuals learn behaviour, and how the process of learning can be systematically and effectively applied as part of a treatment plan. Behaviour therapists believe that all learning occurs in similar ways. In people with problems, a maladaptive pattern of behaviour has been learned, but more adaptive patterns can be learned by the same mechanisms. At first, solutions seemed relatively simple. All that was required to put things right was some modification of the environment – or, in the vocabulary of behaviourism, of the contingencies controlling the behaviours concerned – so that those afflicted learned new, more adaptive responses. Using this model, moreover, many dramatic successes were reported.

As so often happens when new ideas emerge, things proved not to be as simple as at first they seemed. It became clear that patients did not always respond to simple environmental changes in constant, predictable ways. People vary in many ways. They also think. They figure things out and have the power of abstract thought. They do not necessarily have to experience a consequence to a behaviour to reach a conclusion about how the behaviour might turn out. We can also observe and imitate others – the process of modelling – and all these factors, and others, must be taken into account in developing behavioural treatment programmes. We also belong to complex social systems, so that the modification of one person's behaviour is liable to set off a series of changes in the reactions and behaviours of others.

All these considerations have gradually, albeit sometimes grudgingly, been recognised by most behaviour therapists, and they have been – and are still being – incorporated into the practice of behaviour therapy. The intent of this book, however, is to describe and inform, not to argue and convince.

This book is intended, in part, as a further companion volume to *Basic Child Psychiatry* (Barker, 1988). As the editions of that book succeeded one another the author, (Philip Barker) realised that it was not possible to include, in a basic text on child psychiatry, an adequate account of family therapy. The result was the first companion volume, *Basic Family Therapy*. In due course, especially as the cognitive aspects of behaviour came increasingly to the fore, it became clear that this applied also to behaviour therapy. As one reviewer has been kind enough to point out, the behavioural approach to child psychiatric problems is not adequately covered in the latest (5th) edition of *Basic Child Psychiatry*.

The result of the above considerations is this book, which had to be a collaborative enterprise, written along with someone having a special interest in behavioural treatment approaches, (Douglas Murdoch). We hope it provides a clear, easily read, up-to-date and straightforward account of this now quite complex and rapidly evolving field. We have tried to avoid going into too much detail, while setting out the essential points of the various behavioural methods, which apply as much to work with adults as they do to the field of children's disorders. The many references we have included offer the reader guidance as to where more detailed information may be obtained. Nevertheless, we hope that we have provided enough information on behavioural treatment methods to enable the reader to understand the great potential these methods have for resolving many of the problems met with in clinical practice. When we have cited particular patients to illustrate points, their names and some other details have been changed to preserve their anonymity.

Behaviour therapy is but one of the treatments available in the therapeutic armamentaria of mental health professionals. While we have not emphasised its relationship to other therapy methods, it is important to realise that many clinical problems need a comprehensive approach which may involve various other therapies. The all-important process of establishing rapport is also a necessary prerequisite. The fact that it is not emphasised here does not mean that role is not crucial. More on it is to be found in *Basic Family Therapy* (Barker, 1986) and *Clinical Interviews with Children and Adolescents* (Barker, 1990).

Douglas Murdoch
Philip Barker

Chapter 1

What Behaviour Therapy Is and What It Is Not

All behavioural approaches to therapy have as a common aim the direct modification of observable behaviours which have been identified as in need of change. Most behaviour therapists include the verbal reports given by people about their internal experiences and thoughts, and about their feeling states, in their definition of 'observed' behaviour.

These approaches share a common premise, namely that most behaviour is learned according to basic principles of learning – principles which have been established as a result of rigorous scientific study. These principles continue to be elaborated as research continues, both in the laboratory and in applied settings. Behaviour therapists use the most up-to-date understanding of these principles of learning to reduce behaviours that are causing problems and to replace these with more desirable ways of behaving.

Another premise on which behaviour therapy is based is that behaviours serve a function in their current context and are maintained by the events which precede and follow them. These may or may not be the same factors which gave rise to them in the first place. Behaviour therapy therefore addresses those factors that are seen to be maintaining problems rather than those which may have originally caused them to appear. It does not postulate underlying causes, as psychodynamic therapies do, but regards the observed behaviour itself as 'the problem'.

Behaviour therapists attempt to emulate the scientific method in their approach to therapy. In this regard they try to make precise observations of the behaviours of those they treat and to measure accurately the changes that occur as treatment proceeds.

In a review of the treatments of childhood disorders, Mash (1989, page 4) expresses the view that they are best made when:

' . . . they are based on a consistently applied theoretical framework, well established research findings relevant to both normal and deviant child and family functioning, empirically documented treatment procedures, and operational rules that are sensitive to the realities and changing demands of clinical practice. Although such an amalgamation of theory, research and practice is more an ideal than a fact at the present time, current behavioural-systems perspectives seem to approximate this integration most closely . . . '

What makes behaviour therapy unique?

All therapies begin with behaviour. Either the patient or someone in some relationship to the patient expresses a concern (verbal behaviour). If the person expressing the concern is not the patient, then the initiating person will be concerned about some observable problem in the patient's behaviour – either the presence of an undesired behaviour or the absence of a desired one. This is true even when the concern is about some hypothesised internal state such as depression. In these cases, if we ask the person concerned about how they know the patient is depressed (or schizophrenic or 'crazy'), they will inevitably report that the client *does* certain things (or fails *to do* certain things) or says certain things (verbal behaviour). The only way they or we can infer an internal process is through the impact of the client's actions on one or more of our senses or the instruments we use to measure such bodily functions as heart rate, blood pressure and muscle activity.

If the patient is expressing the concern this will be about a behaviour we can observe directly or some internal state that is accessible to us only through the verbal report of the client. In this latter case what we are ultimately treating is the verbal behaviour of the client. Thus we are always dealing with the behaviours of our patients – the concerns they express with their verbal or nonverbal behaviour, or the concerns expressed verbally or in writing by someone else (parents, relatives, officials of government or agents of the legal system). We consider patients cured when their behaviour meets specified criteria; these may comprise samples of behaviour, replies to 'clinical' questions or responses to psychometric assessment measures.

The only way we ever know another person is through his or her overt responses (including physiological measures). As mental health professionals we are always seeking behaviour change; this change may just be the reduction of the patient's complaints or the concerns expressed by the referral source in cases in which we believe the concerns are misplaced. Thus all mental health professionals are 'behaviour modifiers'.

What then is unique about behaviour therapy? The essential point is that it attempts to change the behaviour directly – whether the behaviour be a complex motor response such as shoplifting, or clients' verbalisations of their thoughts, or the behaviour of an organ system, such as within the cardiovascular system when an alteration of blood pressure is sought. The therapy seeks to achieve such changes by using the established principles of learning.

All other therapies attempt to change behaviour indirectly by modifying an underlying system, psychological, biological, or social, that is assumed to cause the behaviour. The essence of the debate between behaviour therapists and therapists of other schools is whether the other theoretical models of how behaviour is acquired, maintained and changed – for example, biochemical explanations or personality theories – are necessary or whether an explanation based on the premise that behaviour is learned through the person's interactions with the environment, according to the known principles of learning, is both a necessary and a sufficient explanation in itself.

We do not aim to extend or resolve the above debate. It has been thoroughly (though not always well) argued in many journals and books (Craighead *et al.*, 1981; Fensterheim and Glazer, 1983; Gardner, 1985; Zeig, 1987). The purpose of this book is to describe behaviour therapy and present it on its own merits and evidence.

But this presents a problem. How does one describe something in the process of change? Behaviour therapy is an evolving system of treatment. Consequently all we can hope to do is to provide a snapshot of where behaviour therapy is as we write, that is, at the beginning of the decade of the 90s.

What is behaviour therapy?

The newcomer to behaviour therapy may be confused by the wide variety of names, many of them quite similar, which are used, often seemingly interchangeably, to describe the field. These include behaviour therapy, behaviour modification, cognitive-behaviour therapy, behavioural psychotherapy, social learning therapy and conditioning therapy. Often there are subtle differences in the therapies being described. For example, the term 'conditioning' is used almost exclusively to describe operant and classical conditioning. 'Behaviour modification' usually, though not always, refers to the use of classical and operant conditioning principles, and excludes any use of modelling or the principles of cognitive change. (These types of therapy are discussed further in Chapter 2.)

'Social learning therapy', 'behaviour therapy' and 'cognitive-behavioural therapies' are terms which generally include the use of cognitive techniques such as the logical analysis of the client's thoughts. But confusion exists here also, because some therapies that are concerned almost wholly with changing the client's internal dialogue and use no operant or classical conditioning techniques are referred to as 'cognitive-behavioural' when in reality they are wholly cognitive. And then there are some therapies which are called 'cognitive' and should be called 'cognitive-behavioural' since they make use of operant and classical conditioning techniques. The best advice we can offer to those of you reading other works in this field is that you should not judge a therapy by its label, but by its content.

In this book, we shall use the term 'behaviour therapy' in its broad definition. This includes the use of all principles of learning whether they be classical, operant or cognitive. With any given client the therapy will usually involve the integration of all three principles. The above approach is the most common. It is reflected in the definition of behaviour modification used by Mahoney, Kazdin and Lesswing (1974) and later by Craighead, Kazdin and Mahoney (1981) which is itself a combination of two earlier definitions. These were:

(1) The use of a broadly defined set of clinical procedures whose description and rationale often rely on the experimental findings of psychological research (Goldstein, Heller and Sechrest, 1966).
(2) The use of an experimental and functionally analytic approach to clinical data, relying on objective and measurable outcome (Goldfried and Pomeranz, 1968, page 14).

The above quotations describe the methodological behaviourism introduced by Watson (1913). We believe that this better describes 'behaviour therapy' than the historically more restrictively used term 'behaviour modification' which has been used to refer simply to the 'application of the principles of operant conditioning' (Skinner, 1953) and/or classical conditioning (Wolpe, 1958).

This view of behaviour therapy regards behaviour as functional or goal orientated. The relevant goals are the observable or reportable consequences of the behaviour which maintain it. Behaviour, which includes thoughts, is therefore a *sample* of the difficulties facing the patient and not merely a *symptom* of the underlying pathology.

The above characteristics of behaviour therapy are well summarised by Mischel (1971). He describes 'three common features':

- Behaviour therapies attempt to modify the problematic behaviours themselves.
- Like the social behaviour theories that guide them, behaviour therapies emphasise the individual's current behaviours rather than the historical origins of his problems.
- Most behaviour therapists assume that deviant behaviour can be understood and changed using the same learning principles that govern normal behaviour.

The scientific emphasis in behaviour therapy

More than anything else, behaviour therapy is an approach that applies scientific methodology, particularly that of the experiment, to the therapeutic enterprise. Science starts with observation, behaviour therapy with assessment (which should contain some form of observation). Science then notes that two or more events tend to occur together or in a predictable way and generates an hypothesis about the relationship. The behaviour therapist also generates hypotheses about the behaviour of concern and events which precede it (called antecedents) and those which follow it (called consequences). Science then tests the hypotheses by specifying independent and dependent variables – those variables which are altered in some way (independent variables) and those variables whose response to the changes in the independent variables are measured (the dependent variables). Behaviour therapy identifies the problem or target behaviour and the antecedents and consequences thought to control the target behaviour. It then changes the antecedents and/or the consequences in a systematic way (independent variables) and measures the change on the target behaviour (dependent variable).

Three other important principles form part of the scientific basis of behaviour therapy:

- Results must be measurable.
- Conclusions should avoid inference and deal only with what has been observed. For example, if when the child is removed from a classroom his screaming stops, the only conclusion that should be reached is that his screaming was related to events in the classroom (that further observation should clarify). No conclusion is warranted that infers that some nonobservable (or reportable) event occurred to stop the screaming, such as the deactivation of an internal conflict concerning mother figures.
- We should use the principle of Occam's razor, namely that only the simplest explanation of the relationship between events should be accepted. In other words, given the choice between two explanations of the available data (observations), one complicated and one simple, both of which adequately explain the observed relationship between events, we should choose the simpler explanation.

In summary, then, behaviour therapy takes an empirical approach to the modification of human functioning. It is empirical in three ways:

- It is based on the results of empirical research conducted using the scientific method.
- It applies the behaviour change principles that have been demonstrated by basic research.
- Its clinical approach uses the scientific method and its applied research must meet the best scientific standards for new findings and techniques to be disseminated and accepted.

One place where behaviour therapy deviates from an ideal science is that it is not based on a single overriding or unifying theory (Craighead *et al.*, 1981). There are well-understood principles, a wide body of well-established facts, and theories about particular aspects of learning and behaviour based upon sound research, but there is no single theory. Nevertheless, there are certain basic assumptions and tenets that underlie behaviour therapy. These may be summarised as follows:

(1) All but the most basic of behaviours are learned.
(2) Maladaptive behaviour is learned by the same principles as is adaptive behaviour.

(3) Maladaptive behaviour can be altered by applying the same basic principles of learning.
(4) The conditions which maintain a behaviour are not necessarily the same as those which created it; therefore the time reference of the therapy is the present, not the historical.

The first principle, that all behaviours are learned, begins with the concept that humans are born with a 'tabula rasa', a blank slate upon which 'experience' (learning) writes its story. This implies that people are products of their environment; there are no inherent drives, behaviours or instincts beyond the basic reflexes. Hence people are neither inherently evil nor inherently good. This principle states that socialisation is the process of teaching culturally relevant and acceptable behaviours and decreasing the presence of socially unacceptable behaviours. Behaviours are learned by their consequences and/or the association of neutral stimuli with stimuli that are capable of eliciting the behaviour. Simple behaviours arise first and are reinforced, punished or have no consequence. If they are reinforced they increase in frequency, duration and/or intensity. If they are punished the behaviours are suppressed, and if they have no apparent consequences they are less likely to occur. Complex behaviours develop as combinations of simple behaviours and/or their modification over time. Hence we see development from a baby's first movements, utterances, smiles and physiological responses, to the complex behaviours of a corporate executive, a surgeon or a microbiologist.

The second principle, that maladaptive behaviour is learned by the same process as adaptive behaviour, is a natural outgrowth of the assumptions of the first principle. If all behaviour is learned and there is no inherent tendency towards acceptable or unacceptable behaviour, then maladaptive behaviour must be acquired and maintained by its consequences just as adaptive behaviour is.

The third principle states that maladaptive behaviour can be changed, and by the application of the same principles of learning that affect all behaviour. Undesirable behaviour can be suppressed by punishment or reduced by taking away the reinforcing consequences. More desirable responses can be achieved by shaping and modelling, and their frequency can be increased through the appropriate use of reinforcement.

The implication of the fourth principle – that the time frame of therapy and the analysis of the behaviour is the current context – is that an understanding of how the behaviour arose in the first place may be of no importance in planning treatment. Consider a boy who has abdominal pain as a result of eating tainted meat and, quite by coincidence, consequently has to stay away from school on the day of a test for which he was poorly prepared. He may then complain of abdominal pain whenever a major test is scheduled. In such a situation, are we going to treat the child for stomach problems, since that is what started the behaviour, or are we going to demand he face the tests he is avoiding, perhaps with the help of remedial tutoring and relaxation training?

In treating adults, behaviour therapists are not primarily concerned with childhood issues. Their concern is the function of the behaviours under study in the adult's current life. Why does that behaviour tend to persist? What are the consequences that maintain it? What does the person gain or avoid by persisting in that behaviour? How can we alter the environment to change those contingencies? Or alternatively, how can we change the person to make more adaptive responses more likely? What skills can we teach that may provide better ways of dealing with difficult situations?

Not all these premises have been borne out in all aspects of behaviour. Therein lie the limitations of behaviour therapy in the minds of many. For example, researchers such as Luria (1961) and Vygostky (1962) and Chomsky (1964) have shown that the acquisition of language occurs too rapidly and in too predictable and consistent a manner to be explained by the principles of operant or classical conditioning. It is also clear that major psychiatric disorders such as schizophrenia and bipolar affective disorders can be neither explained nor cured using learning theory alone.

The roles of biological factors and genetic influences are undeniable in many conditions, even in such common problems as shyness. The first hypothesis is hard to maintain in the light of the current evidence from behavioural genetics (Plomin, 1989) and studies of temperament (Chess and Thomas, 1984). However, despite the desire of some critics who would like to throw out the baby with the bath water, this does not mean that learning theory is incorrect nor that behaviour therapy is not a useful therapeutic approach to many problematic behaviours. What does appear to hold true is that environmental factors (learning) may well determine the degree to which inborn traits are expressed and the particular manner in which they become manifest (Millon, 1986; Plomin, 1989). Indeed, Plomin (1989) has stated that some of the best evidence for the importance of learning comes from behavioural genetics studies which show that despite the previously unrecognised influence of genetics in behaviour, the majority of the influence in human behaviour in most instances still rests with environmental factors.

What makes behaviour therapy different from everyday life?

We all use behaviour modification every day. We thank people for things they do for us. We nag our spouses and our children. We yell at people for injustices to which we feel they have subjected us, and we refuse to give things to people who have previously borrowed items and broken them. In the course of these behaviours we use positive and negative reinforcement, punishment and response cost, four of the mainstay concepts of operant conditioning.

The difference between the applications of learning theory that every one of us uses daily with hardly a thought, and behaviour therapy, is the systematic way in which the latter is planned to bring about more adaptive behaviour in those whose behaviour is in some way less than optimal. It is the systematic application of the principles of learning that distinguishes the practice of behaviour therapy. This involves careful analysis of the relevant variables and precise measurement of changes in behaviour, while the antecedents and consequences of the behaviour are manipulated.

The evolution of behaviour therapy

The roots of behaviour therapy are to be found in ancient Greece. Philosophers such as Aristotle noted that learning occurs when events or stimuli come to be associated. Whether two stimuli became associated with one another was observed to follow certain principles or laws – the laws of contiguity, temporality and similarity.

The modern origins of behaviour therapy are to be found in the basic research on learning and reinforcement that has been carried out in many psychological laboratories, starting in the late nineteenth and continuing throughout the twentieth century. This work began in the laboratory of Ivan Pavlov (1927) in Russia, with his study of the principles of classical conditioning. It was introduced in North America by J.B. Watson (1913) and in the second half of the twentieth century it was subject to explosive growth, beginning with the seminal work on operant conditioning of Skinner (1953). As a method of therapy, its fathers are Joseph Wolpe (1958), Hans Eysenck (1957; 1960), and Ivar Lovaas (1967), among others. In more recent history, major advances can be attributed to Albert Bandura (1969), Mahoney (1974), Beck (1976), Ellis (1958) and Kendall and Braswell (1985). Today, the followers are legion.

In the early days of behaviour therapy, only observable (by an external observer) behaviours and stimuli qualified for manipulation. Hence behaviour therapy was restricted to the manipulation of environmental contingencies. This was because of a desire to keep close to scientific psychology and its roots in the empirical tradition. Today, there is widespread recognition that internal processes (thoughts and feelings) can be behaviours, antecedents and consequences in their own right and mediators of the effects of observable stimuli. Furthermore, there is much evidence that such cognitive stimuli as attributions, beliefs and imagery can be reported in reliable and valid ways by all of us.

Behaviour therapy, like most other therapies, has evolved outside the laboratory as well. It comprises a variety of approaches derived from clinical practice, clinical research, and experimental research with both humans and animals. It is not simply the application of a unified body of knowledge, based on an overriding theory. It is as much an approach, namely the application of the experimental method at the level of the single case.

Chapter 2

Models of Behaviour Therapy

There are three basic models of learning that are used in constructing behaviour therapy protocols; these reflect the evolution of learning theory. The first comprises those approaches which are based on learning or unlearning the association between a stimulus and a response. This is known as classical conditioning. The second model consists of operant conditioning techniques, the essence of which is the planned modification of behaviour through the manipulation of the consequences which follow it. The third model considers the perceptual processes and mental activities of the person. Approaches based on this model are called social learning therapies or, more commonly, cognitive-behaviour therapy.

We will sometimes refer to these models by means of the following symbols:

- Classical conditioning: SR (for Stimulus-Response).
- Operant conditioning: SRC (for Stimulus-Response-Consequence); or ABC (Antecedent-Behaviour-Consequence).
- Social learning theory, or cognitive-behavioural therapy: SORC (Stimulus-Organism-Response-Consequence).

Classical conditioning

The process of *classical conditioning* was the subject of the famous studies in the laboratory of Ivan Pavlov (1927). Pavlov's work showed that reflexive behaviours, such as salivating in the presence of food, could be made to occur using stimuli that did not previously evoke them. He did this by pairing the presentation of the neutral stimulus with the presentation of the stimulus that naturally evoked the reflex. This is the essence of classical conditioning or stimulus response (SR) models of learning and therapy; a stimulus (S) evokes a response (R).

The translation of Pavlov's work into English helped speed the development of behaviour therapy. It inspired the work of one of behaviour therapy's earliest pioneers and most influential authors, Joseph Wolpe, whose book, *Psychotherapy by Reciprocal Inhibition* (Wolpe, 1958), had a major impact on the development of the field.

Classical conditioning starts with two components – a stimulus called the unconditioned stimulus (US), which elicits a reflex, called the unconditioned response or UCR; and a stimulus that does not elicit the UCR. By pairing the presentation of the neutral stimulus with the US, the two come to be associated with one another so that the previously neutral stimulus comes to elicit a response which is nearly identical to the response to the US. It has now become a conditioned stimulus (CS) and elicits a conditioned response (CR). This is usually shown thus:

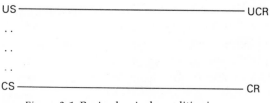

Figure 2.1 Basic classical conditioning.

Once the conditioned response is established it is occasionally necessary to pair the US and CS. If this is not done the strength of the association weakens until the CS no longer elicits the CR. When this happens, the association or learning is said to have undergone extinction.

Some phobias are believed to develop in this way, and the process of extinction is used by behaviour therapists in treating them. A neutral stimulus is paired with a fear-inducing stimulus. The two become associated so that the neutral stimulus now comes to elicit the fear. To 'cure' the phobia, it is necessary to present the CS without the presence of the US. This is the rationale behind the 'exposure' approaches that have proven effective in treating phobias. 'Systematic desensitisation' is the gradual presentation of stimuli more closely approximating the feared (CS) stimulus, while maintaining a state of arousal that is less severe than the CR – usually through the practice of a relaxation technique. 'Flooding' is the sustained presentation of the stimulus until a conditioned reaction no longer occurs.

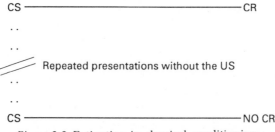

Figure 2.2 Extinction in classical conditioning.

'Aversion therapy' is also based on the principle of classical conditioning. A stimulus is paired with an aversive event. For example, the presentation of alcohol might be paired with the adminstration of an emetic substance. This can lead to the subject feeling nauseated when offered alcohol. This method of treatment tends to raise ethical problems, especially if the aversive stimulus causes discomfort or is painful, as in the case of electric shocks which have been used for this purpose. (We discuss the ethical issues in behaviour therapy in Chapter 15.)

Operant conditioning

The operant model is best understood as the SRC (Stimulus-Response-Consequence) or ABC (Antecedent-Behaviour-Consequence) model. A particular set of antecedent (A) conditions exist during which the person performs a behaviour (B) which is followed by a consequence (C). The consequence will either increase, decrease or have no effect on the likelihood that the behaviour will occur again under similar circumstances. This is sometimes referred to as the functional analysis of behaviour.

As an example, let us take the (fictional) case of eight-year-old Jason. He has learned, through repeated occurrences of the conditions, that when his father is at home (antecedent conditions) his request to stay up late (behaviour) will be rewarded with a yes (consequence). Under this set of conditions, behaviour – namely making a request to stay up an extra half hour – is performed more often.

In operant conditioning we are dealing with probabilities. The behaviour in question is not necessarily performed each time the antecedent conditions exist; nor does the consequence have to occur each time for the behaviour to be maintained. To put it another way, in the presence of the antecedent conditions – father present at bedtime – there might be an 80 per cent chance that Jason will ask to stay up later, because there is a 33 per cent chance that father will reward the request by saying yes. On the other hand, in the presence of other antecedent conditions – mother present at bedtime – the probability of Jason asking to stay up later might be 5 per cent, because the chances that mother will reward the request with a yes are less than 0.5 per cent (she did once when she was too tired to put up with Jason's whining if she said no).

According to this model – operant conditioning – behaviour is determined by its consequences. Antecedent conditions are relevant in so far as the presence or absence of the reinforcer (being allowed to stay up late) is important in determining what will happen. Behaviour is thus functional and goal-orientated rather than reflexive. In its most basic form this model does not need to postulate any cognition or internal processes at all – the person becomes a 'black box' (a box into which one cannot see). The model holds that processes occurring within the individual cannot be subject to objective observation. They are therefore not a fit area for study, nor relevant to the development of a scientifically based therapy. The goal of the behaviour is always the observable external (or measurable physiological) consequence of the behaviour. Sometimes behaviour occurs in random fashion, by pure chance. If the behaviour then becomes associated with a rewarding consequence, and this happens frequently enough, then the behaviour will occur more often and be maintained by the random delivery of the reinforcer. This is how superstitious behaviour arises.

Operant processes are quite pervasive in our lives. We thank people ('positive reinforcement'), stop nagging people when they do what we want them to do ('negative reinforcement'), refuse to lend books to people who don't return them ('response cost') and criticise work we consider sloppy ('punishment').

Social learning or cognitive-behaviour therapy

Our third model of behaviour therapy opens the 'black box' far enough to allow subjects to report on cognitive processes they are aware of in themselves. It also takes into account those internal processes that can be deduced by the therapist from their verbalisations. In this model, we assume that cognitive processes intervene between the stimulus and the behaviour. It is not the stimulus itself which elicits the behaviour but the meaning that the person gives to the stimulus. Consequences are also influenced by cognitions, in that consequences are meaningful because those concerned deem them so. This model can be represented as the SORC model: Stimulus-Organism-Response-Consequence.

The organism (person) mediates between the stimulus, the behaviour and the consequence. We must also be aware that learning can occur without direct reinforcement – learning that can only be explained through cognitive processes such as imitation. In addition to the antecedent and consequent factors considered in the previous two models, we must now consider also the processes of perception, attribution, beliefs, and the influence of cognitive abilities and deficits.

An example of the importance of perception and beliefs is provided by a study of driving behaviour which found that the actual rate at which motorists were caught speeding (the actual probability that one would be caught speeding) had no effect on the number of cars speeding. However, the motorists' perception of the probability that they would be caught did predict driving behaviour.

Another example is afforded by subjects suffering from phobias. They have been shown to estimate the likelihood of aversive consequences (for example, a plane crashing) as being much higher as they approach the feared situation (Beck, 1976).

Cognitive processes are usually referred to as mediating variables. The thoughts themselves are not the causes of the behaviour that follows. The 'cause' of behaviour remains the consequences that will occur if any of the behaviours the person has available are performed and/or the presence of stimuli that elicit learned reflexes. Cognitions are viewed mediating the behavioural response. This is because the perception of the situation influences the choice of the behaviour.

Let us consider the example of a man buying a new suit and wearing it home. How does his wife react? The following sequence of events illustrates the role of cognitive processes. These are printed in italic.

First will come the process of *perception*. Does his wife even *notice* that he is wearing a new suit? Perhaps she has had a hectic day at work herself and is quite *preoccupied*. Her *attention* is *focussed* elsewhere and she *does not notice* the suit. In this case no relevant behaviour is performed because the cue to act is missed. The next question is, does the man *perceive* his wife's lack of response? It is likely that he does, if we *assume* that he was *expecting* his wife to *recognise* his new suit and comment favourably. He now *ponders* her lack of response, *evaluates* it by *remembering* similar past experiences with his wife and others and *comparing* this situation with those. He will evaluate her actions based on his *beliefs* about her and about how people should act in different situations and will probably make some sort of *attribution* about what that behaviour *means* and act accordingly.

This man's reaction to his wife's failure to comment on the suit will vary, depending on the results of his *deliberations*. Let us consider some possibilities. First he could *say to himself*: 'I know from past experience that this is unusual. She will normally say something even if just to tell me I have lousy taste. Something must be bothering her. I had better ask her what's wrong.' He then goes to his wife, puts his arm around her and asks her if anything is wrong because she seems preoccupied.

Another possibility is that he *says to himself*: 'This is the way everybody treats me. They just take me for granted. They never notice me. Even when I really try to look nice for them and be my best, nobody notices. Why should I bother to even try?' He then sags his shoulders, shuffles off to the bedroom, changes and spends the night moping (and leaving his wife *wondering*: 'What's wrong with him?').

Again, he might *say to himself*: 'This is just the way my dad treated my mum. He never *remembered* any important dates, never *noticed* all the things she did for him, never *noticed* when she went to extra effort to look good and all she ever did was take it. Well, I'm not going to take it. Nobody takes me for granted, not even my wife – especially not my wife!' He promptly explodes in a rage that sends his wife fleeing for safety.

Thus we have exactly the same situation but three quite different responses, mediated by the cognitive processes that occurred between the situation and the response.

A comprehensive model

Although the three approaches to behavioural formulations we have described have been presented as three models, in reality they are progressive steps in building a comprehensive model. Current concepts had their origins when it was noticed that certain stimuli could elicit a response. They were elaborated when it was observed that what followed a behaviour (its consequence) was just as important, if not more so. Then it became clear that different people reacted differently, even in the same situation involving the same consequences, and that the differences could be understood, predicted and controlled once we knew the meaning the situation and the consequences had for each person. This development can be summarised as follows:

SR   Stimulus - Response
SRC   Stimulus - Response - Consequence
SORC   Stimulus - Organism - Response - Consequence

We should not regard the above as competing models for understanding behaviour. In reality there is but a single model which has been gradually developed since before the turn of this century – a model of increasing complexity and sophistication, built from the ground up in steady steps. Research continues at all levels of this model. There is currently a veritable explosion of research and new knowledge in the area of cognitive processes and their relevance in altering maladaptive behaviour (Gardner, 1985).

The above should not be taken to mean that there are not those who do see these models as rival and mutually incompatible approaches. Ardent defenders of the position that the study and treatment of behaviour problems should be limited to the respondent and/or operant models have been two of the founders of the behavioural approach, B.F. Skinner and Joseph Wolpe. Skinner has frequently and passionately attacked what he sees as a movement away from a scientific study of human behaviour, namely the addition of cognitive processes to the equation of human behaviour. Skinner stills maintains we should study only what is observable by an independent observer. Since thoughts cannot be directly observed by such an observer, they cannot be a legitimate area of study for a scientific approach to human behaviour (Skinner, 1971).

We must give each of these men his due, for they have made an enormous contribution to our ability to understand, predict and change human behaviour. Furthermore, it is undeniable that we cannot directly observe the thoughts of others. Yet we can know the thoughts of others through observable behaviour, that is, their verbal reports, their marks on questionnaires, and their scribblings in diaries and thought record forms. Moreover, there is ample evidence that these marks, scribbles and verbal productions can and do predict behaviour (Dobson, 1988) and that changing the thoughts that are reported to us (or at least changing the report!) does lead to changes in behaviour (Rush *et al.*, 1977).

We can do no more here than alert you to the fact that a controversy exists. You may become aware of it in your readings, and you should be careful to read beyond the rhetoric and weigh the evidence for yourself – as we all should do when we read the scientific literature. It is, however, safe to say that the majority of researchers and practioners in behaviour therapy today embrace and endorse the position that the inclusion of cognitive processes is both a legitimate and a valuable component of a behavioural approach. While scientific truth should not be decided by a show of hands, a book describing a field of study and an approach to the treatment of behaviour problems should describe that field as it is practised by the majority. In this book, therefore, we will present the full cognitive-behavioural model (SORC) as the current state of the art in behaviour therapy.

Despite the above, we must start with the basics. It is easier to understand the full model when one has first understood its component models. The following chapters will deal with the basic concepts of the field of behaviour therapy, starting with the basic SR model and expanding to the operant (SRC) model. Later chapters will discuss some of the basic concepts that are added to develop the full SORC model.

Chapter 3

Some Basic Aspects of Behaviour

Behaviour therapy is continually evolving. Its evolution has been marked not by radical departures which have overturned previous findings but rather by a process of building upon what has previously been learned. It is like an edifice with secure, established foundations to which new parts are continually added. The foundation consists of sound research findings and established concepts. New findings, concepts and techniques are all the while being added. The purpose of this chapter is to describe the basic foundation. Understanding these basic principles, concepts and definitions is a prerequisite to the study of behaviour therapy, and to any discussion of the practical approaches of behaviour therapists.

Some may picture a behaviour therapist as one who, with minimal verbal interaction, arranges a change in the environment to alter the motor behaviour of a patient. Such a person is more like an engineer or technician than a therapist; and the patient is an object of therapy rather than a participant in it. Behaviour therapy can be like this, but nowadays it rarely is. It is more effective to have the active participation and cooperation of patients, rather than having them be passive recipients of the 'treatment'. Moreover, changing behaviour through verbal communication is generally more effective than relying on strictly nonverbal methods.

Behaviour therapy is about changing behaviour, but before we discuss changing behaviour we must understand what behaviour is. What are its characteristics, dimensions and boundaries?

Behaviour

What do we mean when we say 'behaviour'? The visual image that comes to most people when the word behaviour is mentioned is some type of motor movement through space – running, for example. However, is sitting a behaviour? Is thinking a behaviour? Is talking a behaviour? Are the reponses of the cardio-vascular system behaviours? The answer in each case is yes.

Behaviour is 'everything that the organism does' (Reynolds, 1975). During every moment of our lives we are 'behaving'. We are sleeping, dozing, waking, dreaming, daydreaming, thinking, working, sitting, standing, running, breathing, sweating, pro-ducing gastric acids, performing mental calculations, imagining, planning, evaluating, talking, listening, watching, smelling, touching, adjusting balance, digesting, eliminating and so on, almost endlessly.

In more scientific prose, Wilkening (1973, page 32) has defined behaviour as:

'. . . the observable and recordable goal-directed behaviour of an organism or its parts. Behaviour may be overt (speaking, muscle contraction, blinking, etc.); and/or covert (electronic evidence of thinking); it may be verbal (communicating inten-tionally by words) or nonverbal (communicating by gestures and bodily movements).'

Some would take issue with Wilkening's criterion that be-haviour must be goal directed, partly because whether the be-haviour is indeed goal directed may have to be inferred. Another objection to this criterion is that if some behaviours are not goal directed, this excludes some legitimate targets of behavi-our change (for example, reflexes) from the domain of behaviour therapies; on the other hand, if all behaviour is goal directed (if we assume, for example, that reflex reactions occur to ensure the safety of the organism), it is redundant to add 'goal-directed' as a criterion.

In this book we shall regard behaviour as any action produced by any system of an organism. There is, however, more to be-haviour than this. Behaviour has many characterisitics that are often overlooked when patients' difficulties are being discussed or observed. We will first discuss behaviour's three modalities.

The three modalities of behaviour

Behaviour has motor, affective/cognitive and physiological as-pects, or modalities.

Change in motor behaviour is not the only legitimate object of behaviour therapy. Motor behaviour includes physical actions such as hitting, touching, saying please and thank you. But the physiological reactions of the body are also legitimate targets of therapy; they also follow the same laws of learning – and this applies even to the so-called involuntary nervous system. Modification of the functioning of the 'involuntary' systems, using the principles of learning theory, can be achieved by the technique of biofeedback. The mechanical measurement and display of this technique makes the workings of the involuntary systems more clearly observable, and thus more modifiable. Indeed, the ability of the body's various systems to learn is one of the foundations upon which the emerging field of behavioural medicine is based.

Similarly, our cognitions and affective responses can be altered using methods derived from the principles of learning theory. We all talk to ourselves. We monitor and comment upon the environment and our own actions. Sometimes we are well aware of this self-talk and can easily report upon it. At other times, it is very rapid and on the edge of awareness. We must make an effort to attend to it, in order that we can perceive it. Once it is monitored and reported upon, it can be modified by various techniques, based on the principles of learning. For example, the techniques of thought stopping, covert rehearsal, relaxing imagery and mastery imagery are useful in dealing with obsessive-compulsive disorders.

The treatment of depression provides a good example of the benefits of assessing and treating the three behavioural modalities. Depressed people often display a variety of maladaptive motor responses – for example, excessive crying, psychomotor slowing, lying in bed all day. They also show physiological changes – changes in appetite, sleep disturbance, and decreased sexual desire. They may report feelings of sadness and despair, together with 'negative' thoughts such as: 'I'm a worthless failure because I'm already 35 and I'm not a vice-president of the company yet.' Comprehensive treatment programmes such as those of Beck *et al.* (1979) address all three modalities. Beck's therapy is probably misnamed when it is called cognitive therapy, since some of his behavioural interventions are clearly designed to modify motor and physiological behaviour through behavioural means. It is more accurately described as a cognitive-behavioural approach.

The dimensions of the behavioural modalities

Each of the above three modalities also has three dimensions. These are intensity, frequency and duration.

To illustrate these dimensions, let us use as an example the behaviour of a boy who is banging his head.

Intensity refers to the force with which the child bangs his head against a hard object. A boy who bangs his head by barely touching his head on a mattress does not concern us as much as one who bangs his head against the wall with enough force to cause contusions and a detached retina.

Frequency is the rate at which the behaviour occurs, usually expressed as units of behaviour per unit of time. In our example, we would be more concerned about a boy who hit his head on the wall an average of three times per minute than about one who averaged one bang of his head on a wall per year.

Duration is the length of time the behaviour occurs. In our example, a boy whose episodes of head banging lasted hours or even days would cause us more concern than one whose head banging lasted only a couple of minutes.

In many cases we consider these dimensions intuitively. Thus a boy brought to our attention for 'head banging' who in moments of frustration may tap his head on his pillow once or twice, and in whom this occurs a couple of times a year, will probably not be one we will treat for head banging. We are more likely to explain to the concerned caregiver that it is a not uncommon behaviour, and certainly not pathological, nor a cause for concern. On the other hand, a boy who presents with detached retina and forehead contusions and who is reported to bang his head several times a minute for hours on end if not restrained, will probably quickly be admitted for some form of residential treatment.

Figures 3.1 and 3.2 illustrate the above concepts.

The topography of behaviour

It may be important to assess and modify how a behaviour is performed. The same action can often be carried out in many ways. A child can hold a pencil in many different positions and still make legible letters. The behaviour is writing and the topography of the behaviour is the manner in which the child holds the pencil. Sometimes a change in the topography of the behaviour, such as altering the way the child holds the pencil, will improve the skill with which the task is performed.

When we modify the manner in which a behaviour is performed, we are modifying the topography of the behaviour. An example of the importance of the topography of a behaviour was provided by a case of chronic vomiting in a handicapped boy. He

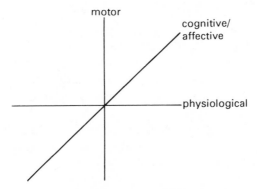

Figure 3.1 Modalities of behaviour.

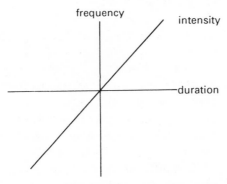

Figure 3.2 Dimensions of behaviour.

was vomiting upwards of 20 times a day for weeks at a time. The behaviour was becoming life threatening due to the resultant electrolyte imbalance, and it was causing great disruption of his family. He also had to be kept in hospital.

Nurses are usually keen observers of behaviour and this proved to be true in this case. They reported that this patient vomited in two different ways. Sometimes he would look 'miserable', be inactive in his bed, and kneel with his head on the mattress. At other times he would be up and active, and the vomiting could occur anywhere in the unit, though usually in the dayroom; he would look around until he caught someone's attention and he then smiled and vomited.

Careful analysis and correlation of data showed that the first topography usually occurred at the onset of vomiting periods and was associated with fever and middle-ear infection. The second topography usually followed and was not associated with any such condition. The first was deemed to be 'medical'. The appropriate response was to treat the middle-ear infection with a suitable antibiotic. The second was deemed 'behavioural'. The behavioural episodes of emesis were thought to be maintained by attention and were dealt with by cleaning the boy up in a rapid, perfunctory way with no verbalisations and minimal or no eye contact. Staff were also instructed to make a point of attending to the child when he was not vomiting. The intervention was successful in reducing the frequency and duration of the vomiting episodes to brief periods lasting only two or three days, with only two or three incidents of vomiting per day and almost always associated with middle-ear infection.

Behavioural repertoires

People do not all do the same things in the same situations. This is what helps make life both interesting and frustrating. Even the same person may display different behaviours in almost identical situations. Indeed, in some circumstances a person's success or failure depends on not always doing exactly the same thing each time. A boxer whose punches are predictable and always come in the same combinations will find himself waking up on the ring floor more often than is good for his health. A soccer player who always uses the same feint and always tries to go the same way around an opposing player will probably have a short professional career. A husband who always produces the same dinner when it is his turn to cook will probably be greeted with groans after a short while.

The behaviours we have available to us in a particular situation comprise our behavioural repertoire. Each behaviour can be assigned a probability – that is, a measure of the likelihood of its occurring in a particular situation. As an example, a tennis player may have six shots in his behavioural repertoire: a lob, a drop shot, cross court, down the line, baseline top spin shot, and an overhead smash. When a return of serve is a high easy volley, his repertoire might be stated as follows:

There is a 40 per cent probability that he will use an overhead smash, a 40 per cent chance of his using a top spin baseline shot, a 10 per cent chance of his going down the line, a 5 per cent chance of a cross court, and a 2.5 per cent chance each that he will use a lob or a drop shot.

Table 3.1 illustrates the above

Table 3.1

Situation	Behavioural repertoire	Probability in situation
High volley return of serve	Overhead smash	40.0
	Lob	2.5
	Down the line	10.0
	Drop shot	2.5
	Cross court	5.0
	Top spin baseline	40.0

These probabilities are not fixed and may change over time, depending on the consequences of each shot. After a while, opposing players are likely to catch on to these probabilities and 'play the odds' quite skilfully, so that they successfully return more shots. The player will probably then change either his repertoire or the probabilities of his current repertoire in order to win the advantage again.

Skill deficits versus performance deficits

People do not always perform the most desirable response in a situation. The tennis player above may fail to place his overhead smash within the court lines. A child may fail to use problem-solving behaviours when faced with frustration. A husband may fail to show affection to his wife.

There are two possible reasons why a person may fail to perform a desirable response in a situation. The behaviour may not be in the person's repertoire. Or it may be that, although the individual is able to perform the behaviour, for some reason he or she does not do so. In other words, there may be either a skill deficit or a performance deficit.

A *skill deficit* is the inability to perform a behaviour in an adequate way. A person may be unassertive because of a lack of the knowledge and behaviours of assertiveness. A person may do poorly in resolving interpersonal conflict because of poor problem-solving abilities. Such individuals cannot describe or demonstrate the ability to perform a skill when asked to do so and have not in the past demonstrated this ability.

A *performance deficit* exists when a person can or has in the past demonstrated the ability to perform the appropriate behaviours but fails to do so when the situation calls for them.

When there is a skill deficit, the first therapeutic task is for the person to acquire the requisite behaviours. When there is a performance deficit, the therapeutic task is either to increase the frequency of the reinforcement of the appropriate behaviour and/ or remove any obstacles, such as anxiety, that may be hindering the performance of the skill.

To illustrate the above, we may consider three children who fail to complete mathematics tasks. The first child may do so because he lacks the necessary skills and, despite trying, cannot complete the work. The therapeutic goal is the acquisition of the specific mathematical skills, probably by means of skilled remedial teaching. The second child may be able to do the work in record time in your office when offered a reward of two tickets to the next professional sports event in town, but may fail to do so at school or at home because achievement is not rewarded, and perhaps not even recognised, in those situations. The therapeutic task is then to alter the reinforcement contingencies to increase the likelihood that the work will be done. This may be achieved either by means of a parent training programme or through the use of family therapy.

The third child may be able to do the mathematical tasks in daily lessons but fail to complete enough questions to obtain a passing grade in a test situation. The problem here may be test anxiety and the therapeutic task then is the reduction of such anxiety.

Distinguishing between the above three types of problem is an essential first step in analysing any school-related problems. It can be frustrating for both child and therapist if errors are made. Thus if a child is assumed to have a performance deficit when in fact she has a skill deficit and is being asked to do something she cannot do, treatment will fail. She is also likely to suffer further emotional trauma as a result.

Chapter 4

Changing Behaviour

The acquisition of new behaviours

We must now look in more detail into how we may change behaviour, decrease problem behaviours and increase desired behaviours that are occurring at too low a rate.*

Unless an individual is able to perform a behaviour the question of increasing or decreasing its rate does not arise. If a desired behaviour is not in a person's repertoire, steps must be taken to enable the subject to acquire it. Sometimes this will be all that is necessary to eliminate a clinical problem. Indeed, the acquisition and reinforcement of a more desirable behaviour, and one that is incompatible with the undesired behaviour, is often a good clinical strategy. So if a child is rude to adults, teaching the child a more polite manner of interacting and then only responding when addressed politely can be an effective way of decreasing the rude behaviour.

Certain fundamental concepts underlie the behaviour therapist's approach to the task of helping a person acquire a new behaviour. These are the concepts of consequences and, most specifically, of reinforcement.

Positive and negative reinforcement

A 'reinforcer' is defined as anything which, when it follows a behaviour, increases the likelihood that the behaviour will be repeated in the future.

*Much research, and many publications, support and amplify the material in this chapter. It is not possible to cite all the work that has been done in the field. The primary references are Craighead, Kazdin and Mahoney (1981); Hulse, Deese and Egeth (1975); Reynolds (1975); Kaplan (1986); Martin and Pear (1983); and Azaroff and Reese (1982). To avoid tedious repetition they will not be cited in the text that follows.

Reinforcement can occur in either of two ways. One is for something to be presented to the person following the performance of the behaviour; the other is for something to be taken away. If something is presented and the behaviour increases, then positive reinforcement is said to have taken place. 'Positive' in this case does not imply any subjective evaluation of the quality of whatever is presented; it simply refers to the fact that something is presented. It might almost be better to call it reinforcement by application or reinforcement by presentation – except that the term 'positive reinforcement' has such an established place in the literature.

If something is taken away and the behaviour increases, then negative reinforcement is said to have occurred. Again, 'negative' does not refer to the subjective quality of the stimulus that has been removed but to the fact of its absence.

To summarise, *positive reinforcement* is the increasing of a behaviour by a subsequent stimulus that becomes *present*. *Negative reinforcement* refers to the situation in which a behaviour increases when a following stimulus becomes *absent*. The catch phrases to remember are – 'present – positive' and 'absent – negative'. Figure 4.1 illustrates this.

There are two reasons why we do not give any subjective value to a 'positive' reinforcer. At first sight it might seem that all, or at least most, such stimuli would be desirable, attractive or providing pleasure. But in reality whether a stimulus is pleasant depends on the person, not on the nature of the stimulus. Thus while most people might consider chocolate to be a 'positive reinforcer' because it is 'delicious', some dislike chocolate. Its contingent presentation following a behaviour to such people might not therefore increase the likelihood of the behaviour being

Effect on future behaviour / Environmental event following target behaviour	Stimulus presented	Stimulus removed
Target behaviour increases	Positive reinforcement	Negative reinforcement
Target behaviour decreases	Punishment by application	Response cost

Figure 4.1 Reinforcement/Punishment Matrix.

repeated. In such a situation, chocolate is not a reinforcer. Thus reinforcers are specific to the individuals being reinforced. It is not possible to know in advance what will be a reinforcer. Indeed, sometimes even the self-report of the subject can be misleading.

The second reason why we do not ascribe inherent value to reinforcers is that a stimulus which is regarded as unpleasant by both an external observer and the subject may prove to be a reinforcer. Consider the case of a parent yelling at a child. It might seem unlikely that children would perform behaviours in order to get their parents to yell at them. Yet sometimes parents' yelling does prove to be the reinforcer maintaining particular behaviours. A child may report not liking the parent yelling and may express the wish that the yelling would stop, yet may persist in the very behaviour that makes the parent yell. The astute and aware youngster might be able to report something to the effect that while the yelling is aversive it is better than not being recognised at all.

Sometimes people refer to goals which are in some way undesirable as the 'lesser of two evils'. The 'necessary evil' may be a positive reinforcer. This will be so if it increases the probability we will perform the behaviour. The following case, seen in consultation by one of us (Douglas Murdoch), demonstrates this:

A father complained that his eight-year-old daughter, Amy, who had been 'wonderful' during a prolonged and serious illness of her brother, was now 'being bad.' I asked him to elaborate. Paraphrased, he said:

'Well, I come home from work and I'm just exhausted. All I want to do is relax and read the paper. Amy usually greets me nicely enough and starts playing on her own. Well, in no time at all she's bothering me, asking me questions and tugging on my newspaper. She won't give me any peace.'

I asked him what he did when Amy asked him questions. He replied:

'Well, at first, I try to be nice and answer briefly and then go back to reading my paper.'

'Then what happens?' I asked.

'She just keeps pestering me with questions.'

'Then?' I persist.

'I get angry and yell at her to stop bothering me.'

'And?'

'She stops and goes back to playing with her dolls or whatever but in no time she has another question or starts singing or something else that's irritating.'

'What do you do then?' I ask.

'I have to put the newspaper down and give her a lecture on respecting my quiet time.'

'What does Amy do then?'

'She starts to argue with me which isn't like her at all and before I know it I've wasted 20 minutes, dinner's ready and I haven't got my paper read.'

My advice to Amy's father was that he stop for 25 minutes or so at a coffee shop on the way home from work. While there he should read his newspaper and relax. When he got home he should greet his daughter as usual. He should then start talking to her or playing with her, whenever she was playing nicely by herself (reinforcing an incompatible behaviour already in Amy's repertoire); and he should ignore Amy or give neutral answers ('I'm busy just now, go and play and I'll be with you in a minute') when she tried to gain his attention through the use of irritants.

I telephoned Amy's father two weeks later and once again his daughter was 'wonderful'.

'Has this problem got better or worse or stayed the same lately?'

'It's been getting worse.'

Clearly, Amy was working hard to get her father to yell at her. It seemed that, for her, any attention from her father was better than no attention at all. She seemed to be in a severe state of deprivation, probably because she had been deprived of her parents' attention for five years during her brother's long illness. In this example, the antecedent condition was the father's ignoring of Amy, her bothering him was the 'behaviour' and his reprimands were the consequences.

Amy used many of the behaviours in her repertoire to bring about the consequence she wanted, namely having her father attend to her. Since his attention (answering, yelling, arguing) followed her behaviour and the behaviour was increasing, we may conclude that his attention was a positive reinforcer since it was applied contingent to the behaviour and resulted in increased frequency, intensity and duration of the behaviour.

Negative reinforcement is the contingent removal of a stimulus when a desired behaviour is performed. A good example is nagging. A wife nags her husband to take out the rubbish. Grumbling, he takes it out and the nagging stops (removal of a stimulus – nagging – contingent on a particular behaviour). If the likelihood that the husband takes out the rubbish on future occasions increases, then the nagging is a negative reinforcer.

Most of us would consider praise to be a pleasant event and hence likely to be a positive reinforcer. Yet some people will decrease the contingent behaviour upon the presentation of praise and increase the frequency of behaviours that terminate praise. When this happens, praise is a negative reinforcer. For example, a teenage boy whose mother praises him excessively may increase the frequency of those behaviours which lead to a reduction in how often his mother praises him, when he is in the presence of his new 'in' friends.

What we call the various behaviours occurring in an interaction between two or more people depends on our perspective. A child's behaviours will be the stimuli (antecedent and consequence) to the mother's behaviour. At the same time the child perceives the mother's behaviour as the antecedents and consequences of his or her behaviour. An observer will assign the terms depending on whose behaviour is the target of modification. Children modify their parents' behaviour just as much as parents modify their children's behaviour.

An example of the latter process is an account given by a six-year-old child who in an informal interview gave what could only be termed a treatise on how to modify her mother's behaviour using contingent responses. She described sequences of behaviour such as (paraphrased): 'If I want something, I'll ask my mum. Sometimes she says yes but other times she'll say no, especially if she's in a bad mood. If she says no then I get angry and yell at her, calling her mean. Sometimes that works and she gives me what I want so then I'm nice to mum. Sometimes that doesn't work though and she sends me to my room. Then I cry and say how sorry I am. That works almost every time because mummy doesn't like me to cry and then she gives me what I want.'

The following sequence of behaviours demonstrates how the use of the terms antecedent, behaviour and consequence depend on who is the identified patient and also at what point in a sequence of behaviours one starts:

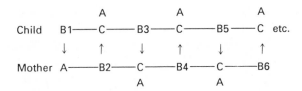

The child's first action (B1) is also the antecedent (A) to the mother's first action (B2) which in turn is both the consequence (C) of the child's first action and the antecedent to the child's second action (B3) which in turn is both the consequence of the mother's first act and the antecedent of her second (B4) and so on.

Developing behaviours

Many techniques are available for addressing behavioural deficits. The simplest is shaping or successive approximation, but there are other, more efficient ways, depending on the behaviour to be acquired and the abilities of the client.

Shaping or successive approximation

A man aiming to create a sculpture begins with a block of stone bearing no resemblance to the work of art he hopes to create. He does not make a single tap of the hammer and create a finished product. He first chips away to give the block a rough form closer to the shape he eventually hopes to achieve. He keeps chipping away until gradually the shape comes closer and closer to the final form he has in mind. Eventually, he is carefully putting the finishing touches to his sculpture.

The process of shaping is similar. First, we reinforce any action that even vaguely resembles the behaviour we are trying to increase, even if the performance appears accidental. We then only reinforce behaviours that are a little closer to the target behaviour. As the behaviour continues to move closer and closer to the target behaviour, we only reward successively closer steps until we are refining the nuances of the behaviour. A simple behaviour might be quite rapidly shaped. A complex behaviour might take years to develop.

Modelling

A more rapid method by which higher organisms acquire a behaviour is by means of modelling. Bandura (1969) conducted some landmark experiments that helped set the foundation for social learning theory. He demonstrated that children will perform new behaviours with no shaping and no reinforcement through the use of imitation. The children first observed a person perform a unique behaviour which they had not previously demonstrated (such as kicking a rubber life-sized doll that has a round bottom and will bounce back upright when hit). They were not instructed to imitate the behaviour nor were they shaped to perform the same action, but when provided with the opportunity they imitated the behaviour completely.

Modelling may be defined as a process of learning whereby a person acquires a new response through the observation of that behaviour being performed by another person (or organism) and then repeating the response without further instruction or training.

Most of us have used modelling almost without thinking. We realise that the quickest and often the best way to teach a person a new skill is to demonstrate the skill. So we do a mathematics problem and speak aloud each of the steps; or we get down on a tumbling mat and do a somersault. The person we are demonstrating the skill to may be able to do a reasonable copy on the first try. If we had tried to teach a maths skill or a tumbling technique by the principles of reinforcement and shaping alone, waiting for a random first approximation, it might have taken an inordinately long time. There is no way our education system could teach as much as it does in the space of 15 to 20 years.

Modelling is a powerful and efficient means whereby people may acquire new behaviours. Perhaps nowhere is this better understood than in the advertising industry which makes extensive use of the principles of modelling. It is because of what we know about the effects of modelling that there is much controversy over the amount of violence portrayed on television. It is perhaps unfortunate that children see many violent acts committed not only by the villians but also by the heroes of TV shows.

There are many factors that determine how likely it is that a behaviour will be modelled. Among these, the characteristics of the model are critical. One quality of the model that is important is the similarity between the model and the person doing the modelling. The closer the model is in age, sex, skill level, nationality, ethnic and almost any other characteristic, the more likely the person is to imitate the model. Advertising professionals recognise this by picking as representatives to present their products models whose characteristics are close to those of the population they hope will purchase the products being advertised. In North America, the advertisements for beer provide superb examples of this. Different brands target different audiences. The popular local brands are often presented being used by either young to middle-aged men engaged in the recreational pursuit of sports or watching professional sports, or by young men and women enjoying the beverage at a social gathering at which they are obviously having fun. Premium beers, especially imports, are shown being consumed by more 'sophisticated' models who are dressed more expensively, are seen in more affluent surroundings, and are engaged in quieter pursuits such as listening to a top-of-the-range stereo system.

The attractiveness of the model also influences the amount of modelling that occurs. The more attractive the model, the more likely it is that the model's behaviour will be copied. This also is well understood in the advertising industry which seeks always to present attractive people engaging in the behaviour they want the consumer to copy (usually the purchase and consumption of a product). Since attractiveness is in the eye of the beholder, once again the target audience is critical. For example, as the black population of the United States has become more affluent, there has been an increase in the number of attractive black models used in advertisements. Expensive products tend to be shown used by tall, elegant, attractive, richly dressed middle-aged models, especially film stars. Products targeted to a younger and less affluent audience are shown being used by attractive, casually dressed young people.

Another key factor is whether the model displays mastery or coping and what the observer's skills are in this dimension. A mastery model is a model who has mastered the skill in question and displays it with a high degree of competence. A coping model is a model caught in a dilemma similar to that of the observer; the latter may acquire the behaviour as a way of solving the dilemma. The model may give a 'before and after' demonstration.

Yet another factor, especially when the model is in an active relationship with the person acquiring the behaviour, is how nurturing the model is perceived to be. A model who is warm, caring and empathetic, and has a history of being able to meet many of the observer's (or other people's) instrumental and/or emotional needs, will be copied more often than a model seen as cold, insensitive, strident or prone to withhold emotional resources. This, no doubt, is why many hold Mother Theresa up as a model. It is also why the image of behaviour therapists as cold and impersonal technicians is a poor one. Such persons are poor behaviour therapists because they fail to demonstrate the qualities which make clients more likely to model their example.

The power held by the model is another important factor. The degree to which the model is perceived to have power – to administer meaningful rewards and punishments – will influence the degree to which that model is copied.

Finally, the consequences to the model are important. A model who is punished is unlikely to be copied whereas a model who is rewarded will be copied.

Instruction

We are not restricted to the use of demonstration for the efficient acquisition of new behaviour. If we were, we would all leave our current training institutions and take our instruction from Marcel Marceau. Fortunately, we are verbal creatures and can use our verbal skills to help others acquire new behaviours. Thus we can instruct our clients how we think they should or could behave in particular situations. We can describe what we want them to do and use verbal feedback in the shaping process.

Learning curves versus 'all-or-none' learning

Behaviour can be acquired at different rates depending on factors such as the complexity of the behaviour to be learned, the amount and specificity of the feedback provided, the motivation for learning (which is related to the amount and type of reinforcement), the opportunities for learning, the ability of the person to acquire new learning and any handicapping conditions that may exist. The acquisition of a behaviour will usually follow a curve, with an early and rapid improvement in the skill with which the new behaviour is performed. There is then a slowing of the rate of improvement, with a levelling out when the person is approaching the limit of his or her ability, such that it takes greater effort and more time to make fewer gains.

The above phenomenon is well illustrated in the acquisition of athletic skills. A newcomer to, say, the high jump may achieve a height of four feet at the first try. By the end of the first month of training, with the benefit of a coach who understands the concepts of shaping, modelling, reinforcement, feedback and instruction, the new athlete may be able to jump four feet, six inches. By the end of the first year of training, six feet may be achieved, seven by the end of the third and then, even with optimal training conditions, with the best coaches available and daily attention to practice using all the principles of acquiring new responses, the athlete may only add a few inches to the height jumped each

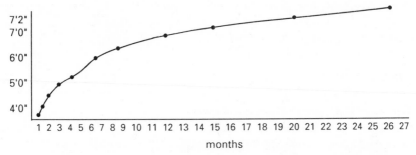

Figure 4.2 An example of a learning curve: high jump skills.

year, though those few inches might be considered extremely significant. Figure 4.2 illustrates this.

Occasionally, due either to the nature of the response or to the existence of optimal conditions for learning, a response may be acquired in an 'all-or-none' fashion. This is termed 'one-trial learning'. Examples are the learning of emotional reactions to neutral stimuli associated with a traumatic experience – such as a fear of buses after being assaulted while travelling on one.

Insight and problem solving

It may seem strange that the term 'insight' is included in a text on behaviour therapy. Has there, you may wonder, been a glitch in the word processing program so that a segment of a text on psychoanalysis has become intermixed with the current text? No, this has not happened. 'Insight' in this case is not used as psychoanalysts use the word – for the understanding of repressed personality dynamics – but rather for the 'aha' experience documented in the literature, particularly in relation to scientific thinking. We are referring here to the sudden awareness of as-sociations or solutions to behavioural difficulties that leads to new responses. 'Problem solving', on the other hand, refers to the systematic analysis and resolution of difficulties. The subject thinks the problem through in order to develop new responses which may lead to resolution of the problem.

Prompts

Prompts include cues, instructions, physical guiding (a great technique for comedy films in which the golf professional is able to wrap his arms around the beautiful leading lady to show her how to swing the club properly), gestures, directions and giving examples. Models may also act as prompts. If a prompted be-haviour is reinforced, it may soon be possible to fade the prompt and the behaviour will persist.

Chaining

We are often presented with clients who need to learn a whole sequence of skills in order to be more adaptive. Or a client may have the requisite skills but fail to put them together in an adaptive sequence. The procedure we use in such situations is called 'chaining'.

In chaining, two or more responses are required, in the correct sequence, in order for the reinforcement to be delivered. Chains are usually quite simple at first; they are then built up step by step until the person is able to perform long sequences of behaviours to obtain the reward. The acquisition of mathematical skills is in many ways a chained set of responses, done in a specific sequence, to obtain the reinforcers (the right answers and whatever extrinsic reinforcers may be the reward for the correct answers).

In the case of mathematics, the process of building the chain takes years. It starts by reinforcing the most basic first step – recognition of numerical values ('How many fingers have you got, Timmy?'; 'How many noses have you got, Sally?') and then adds skills in basic operations (addition, subtraction, multiplication, division). Next come problem-solving skills (if Mary has two lollipops and Johnny has three lollipops, how many lollipops have they got?), and rules of sequential operations. The Nobel prize physicist has developed the ability to use very long chains of mathematical responses together to obtain reinforcements (correct answers, peer recognition, salary, prizes and awards, research grants, graduate student assistants, requests for speaking engagements and so on).

An example of the use of chaining might be the process of teaching our daughter to go to the shop to buy milk. First when she is still quite young, we take her into the shop and let her get the milk out of the refrigerator. We then tell her what a big help she is. We smile and give her a hug. Another time, we let her get the milk out of the refrigerator and carry it to the counter before we give her the smile, the thanks and the hug. Next, we let her do these two things, then hand over the money, and then we deliver the reinforcer. The next step might be giving the child the right money and sending her into the shop while we wait in the car. The chain preceding the reinforcer is now: go into the shop; find where the milk is kept; get the right size and type of milk; take it to the counter; pay for it; bring it out to the car.

As we continue to build the chain, we can add components such as getting money from the household money envelope, counting the correct change, riding a bicycle or walking to the shop, making a shopping list, getting a variety of items from the same shop, getting a variety of items from several shops and so on.

Strengthening existing behaviours

The acquisition of a behaviour is merely a first step. It is still necessary to ensure that the behaviour occurs at the right frequency, intensity and duration, and in the correct situations. This is the task we must consider next. It may be our first task if the client is already able to perform the behaviour but fails to do so with sufficient strength or in the right situations. The most common and effective means of accomplishing this is to alter systematically the reinforcement contingencies.

We will concentrate on increasing the frequency of a response in order to avoid the tedium of constantly repeating frequency, intensity and duration; however, the principles to be explained can also be used to cause an increase in the intensity and duration of responses (for example, using reinforcement to help singers increase the projection of their voices and their ability to sustain a note).

The concept of reinforcement has been defined in the section on the acquisition of new responses. We must now consider how behaviours are reinforced. This involves the schedules which determine when a behaviour will be reinforced and their alteration to increase the frequency of a behaviour and maintain a response.

Schedules of reinforcement

When we are trying to get the client to acquire a new behaviour, we reinforce almost every occurrence of the behaviour. Once it is established, a behaviour is usually reinforced only part of the time. This is referred to as intermittent reinforcement. The term 'schedules of reinforcement' refers to the rules determining when a reinforcer will be delivered. This can be on the basis of time or rate of response (interval versus ratio). Reinforcers can be delivered in a predictable, consistent manner or they can be delivered in an inconsistent manner (fixed versus variable schedules). These patterns can also be combined.

The simplest schedule is that of reinforcing a behaviour every time it occurs. This is referred to as a 'fixed ratio one schedule' (FR 1). It is fixed because the reinforcer is delivered after an exact number of responses (every one). It is a ratio schedule because the delivery of the reinforcer is determined by the *number* of responses. This is an easy schedule to administer and is used extensively when helping people to acquire new responses, or to cause an immediate increase in the rate at which a behaviour is performed. However, this schedule has little resistance to extinction. Almost as soon as the reinforcer is no longer being delivered, the behaviour begins to drop off. Another problem is that it involves a large amount of reinforcement in a short time. This may lead the person to become satiated on the reinforcer which then loses its effectiveness. It then becomes necessary either to switch to a new reinforcer or to take a break.

One solution to the above problem is to require more responses before delivering the reinforcer. One might reinforce only after every fifth response, for example. This would be a fixed ratio five schedule (FR 5). Again it is fixed, since the reinforcer is *always* delivered after *exactly* the same number of responses. It is a ratio since it is based on the *number* of responses (five responses). This is more resistant to extinction and hence a response that is maintained on an FR 5 schedule is said to be more *robust* than a response maintained on an FR 1 schedule. One could increase the robustness of a response by continuing to increase the number of responses required over time, a concept called *fading of reinforcement*. There are also other means of increasing the robustness of responses.

Reinforcers do not have to be delivered after exactly the same number of responses every time and in 'real' life they rarely are. They can be delivered after three responses one time, seven the next time and five the time after that so that on *average* the reinforcer is delivered every fifth time. This is referred to as a variable ratio of reinforcement since the ratio varies around an average. These schedules of reinforcement are much more robust than are the equivalent fixed ratio schedules, probably because they are less predictable. The two are shown graphically in Fig. 4.3.

Reinforcement does not have to be delivered according to the

Fixed ratio 4
(FR 4)

```
        R               R               R               R
B—B—B—B—B—B—B—B—B—B—B—B—B—B—B—B—B—B—B
        R               R       R       R
```

Variable ratio 4
(VR 4)

B = One instance of the behaviour
R = Reinforcement delivered

Figure 4.3 Examples of fixed and variable reinforcement schedules.

frequency of responses. It can also be based on time. In this case, the first behaviour following a specified time period is reinforced. On a 'fixed interval one minute' schedule, for example, the first response to be performed after one minute has elapsed will be reinforced. Interval schedules can also be fixed or variable, just as ratio schedules can be. A fixed interval five minute schedule would mean that exactly five minutes after the last reinforcer was delivered, the next reinforcer becomes available. A 'variable interval schedule – five minutes' would mean that the next re-inforcement would be available on average five minutes after the last reinforcer was delivered, so that sometimes it would be available one-and-a-half minutes after the last reinforcer, some-times seven minutes after, sometimes four minutes after and so on.

Bus timetables provide us with examples of interval schedules of reinforcement and their effect on behaviour. Imagine, if you will, observing two bus stops during a morning commuting period. At one of these, service is provided precisely every 15 minutes starting on the hour. This would be a fixed interval 15 minute schedule (FI 15) – the behaviour being standing at the stop, the reinforcer being the bus. What you would observe is that people would approach the stop very close to each quarter hour and there would be very few people standing at the stop at any other time. (If you interviewed anybody who was standing at the stop at, say, eight minutes past the hour, you would prob-ably find out that they were new users who did not know the timetable.)

At the second stop, a very irregular service is provided so that on average a bus arrives at the stop every 15 minutes (variable interval 15 or VI 15). But sometimes two buses arrive within seconds of one another and at other times there is 30 minutes between them. What you would now observe is that there are almost always people at the bus stop, with a slightly higher concentration of people close to each quarter hour. If we observe the behaviour of a single commuter, we will probably see that a commuter using the first service (fixed interval) will leave his or her home at almost the same time every day and arrive at the bus stop within a very narrow range of time just before a quarter hour, spending very little time engaged in the behaviour 'stand-ing at the bus stop'. A commuter using the second service (vari-able interval) is likely to leave home at more irregular times, will arrive well before the quarter hour but with much more vari-ability, and spend a much greater amount of time engaged in the behaviour 'standing at the bus stop' (and the secondary be-haviours of angry rumination about bus companies and verbal complaints to fellow commuters). Figure 4.4 illustrates these two schedules.

The behaviour of children in a classroom is often maintained on interval schedules. Breaks and the finish of school are on fixed interval schedules such that the behaviour 'lining up at the door' will be observed very close to breaktime, lunch and the end of the school day. The behaviour 'raising one's hand for assistance during a lesson' will probably be maintained on a variable interval schedule. The variation will be around the average amount of time the teacher spends assisting each child. Sometimes she may spend only 30 seconds, sometimes several minutes, during which time her assistance is unavailable to the other students. Hands will start to go up the closer the interval approaches that teacher's 'average' interval of unavailability.

In the classroom which the children in our inpatient unit attend we sometimes use these schedule effects to reduce 'raised hands' behaviour. We shift the child from a variable interval schedule of reinforcement (which maintains a high rate and/or duration of the behaviour) over to a fixed interval schedule. ('I've just finished helping you. I will come to help you if you raise your hand five minutes from now, but not before.') Television-watching and attending therapy sessions are often interval-determined behav-iours (though some clients expect that therapy will be delivered on an FR 1 schedule – whenever they show up, appointment or not!).

The main difference between the ratio and interval schedules

	7:00	7:03	7:06	7:09	7:12	7:15	7:18	7:21	7:24	7:27	7:30
Fixed interval 15 minutes { *					10	85	5				
†						100					
Time	7:00	7:03	7:06	7:09	7:12	7:15	7:18	7:21	7:24	7:27	7:30
Variable interval 15 minutes { † 3	3	3	4	8	16	32	16	8	4	3	3
*		5	10	15	25	30	10	5			

† = the percentage of times standing at stop will be rewarded with the arrival of the '7:15' bus.

* = the percentage of time a particular commuter will be observed standing at the bus stop at that moment.

Figure 4.4 Fixed and variable interval schedules.

is that when interval schedules are in effect, the number of responses does not matter. The amount of time since the last reinforcer was available is the critical factor. In ratio schedules, the number of responses is the critical factor and the time it takes is irrelevant. In an FR 5 schedule, the fifth response will be reinforced whether it occurs within five seconds or five hours of the last reinforced response.

Compound schedules

Schedules can be combined in three different ways to create different effects:

(1) They can be combined so that only one of the schedules needs to be satisfied for a reinforcer to be delivered.
(2) The reinforcer may be delivered only when all the requirements are met.
(3) Reinforcement may be delivered when the requirement of certain combinations of subsets of multiple schedules are met. For example, one can mix an interval responding schedule with a ratio schedule so that a reinforcer is delivered only when a specified number of responses have occurred and a specified time period has elapsed since the last reinforcer.

People may work on quota systems in which the reinforcer (a pay bonus, for example) is only given at set intervals (for example, weekly) and only if the quota has been achieved or exceeded in this time period. This is called a conjunctive schedule of reinforcement. If the reinforcer is delivered when either of the component schedules has been met, this is an alternative schedule of reinforcement; thus a reinforcer is delivered after the first response which follows a specified elapsed time since the last reinforcer *or* following a specified number of responses regardless of elapsed time.

School advancement might follow this schedule. Thus children would pass either when they have completed enough work with enough skill to meet the frequency (ratio) requirements; or after they have spent a set amount of time in a class (for example, two years) regardless of their academic standing. The complexity of these schedules can be enormous and hence may defy analysis. Further and more detailed explanations are to be found in texts on learning theory. (An excellent short and precise one is *A Primer of Operant Conditioning* (Reynolds, 1975).)

One problem with developing and enhancing new adaptive behaviours is that they have a tendency to occur only within the treatment setting. A shy child who learns to ask for help when needing it at home may still sit quiet and helpless when faced with a difficulty at school, in a restaurant or with friends. We say that the behaviour has failed to generalise. Failure to generalise is due to the tendency for reinforcement to be associated with antecedent events that signal the availability of the reinforcer. Thus the antecedent stimuli (a parent or the physical surroundings of the house or both) are missing in each of the other situations. Generalisation is developed by reinforcing the behaviour in a wider variety of settings. In the example above, the next step would probably be a school conference to transfer the reinforcement programme to that setting as well. In addition, the parents may take the child to a variety of physical settings and encourage the child to make requests which can then be reinforced. The same parents may also bring neighbours and relatives into the plan so that the reinforcement is increasingly associated with a wide variety of stimulus situations.

Another problem is that behaviour changes tend not to persist. This is a failure of maintenance and usually means that the reinforcement schedule was thinned (requiring more responses to obtain the reinforcer) too quickly and an extinction procedure was accidently initiated. One obvious solution is to reinstate the reinforcement schedule on a richer basis (fewer responses required per reinforcer, or less time between available reinforcers on an interval schedule). One problem with this is the potential cost to the environment (parents'/teachers' time, material resources). A solution is for subjects to take responsibility for their own reinforcement – a major step in the development of self-control.

Another key concept is 'habit strength'. A well-learned, or even overlearned, response that has been practised repeatedly while the reinforcement has been slowly thinned will maintain itself a long time with minimal additional reinforcement. This is especially important in the development of a new response to a situation that already has a well-developed maladaptive response with considerable strength of its own.

Reducing behaviours

The reduction or elimination of an undesired behaviour is a common request of new clients seeking help. The undesired behaviour may include internal events such as sad affect – that is, sadness of mood – or the excessive production of gastric acids.

A variety of methods is available to reduce the frequency of undesired behaviours. Punishment comes quickly to mind. Certainly, this is the case when many parents and teachers are faced with a child's misbehaviour. Their request of you may well be to suggest a more effective form of punishment. This is unfortunate since punishment is not always the most effective way and has many potentially serious side effects. Nevertheless, let us start by looking at it.

Punishment: by application and response cost

Punishment by application is the presentation of a stimulus after a response such that the probability that the response will be performed under similar circumstances is decreased. It is an operational definition in that it defines the operation necessary to determine if a stimulus is a punishing stimulus or not. You present your chosen stimulus following a response and see if the response decreases along one or more of the three dimensions of behaviour – frequency, intensity or duration. That is the only way to determine if it is a punishing stimulus.

A good example was the common practice in North American schools in the 1950s and 1960s of administering a painful slap across the palm of the hand with a wide belt referred to as the 'strap'. This was considered a punishment and in many cases it resulted in a decrease in the frequency of the problem behaviour and hence would qualify as a punishing stimulus. But some children's misbehaviour did not decrease after 'getting the strap'. In some cases, children even behaved in ways that ensured they would get the strap (hence it was a reinforcer – increasing the probability of a behaviour). In such cases, the strap may have been a 'badge of courage', that proved they were not afraid of or were not giving in to authority. It is also possible that unresponsive children had become accustomed to the strap from repeated administrations so that it no longer had any effect on them (habituation – one of the dangers of punishment). With these children, the school personnel were presenting a painful stimulus but were not punishing a behaviour. This may be especially true if the strap is simply one stimulus in a behaviour chain that results in a reward.

As an example, consider the case of a boy who is taunted by a peer. He then hits the peer – and is next taken to the school principal who administers the strap. The boy goes home and tells dad, who praises him for standing up for himself; he then tells his son, for the hundredth time, how tough he was as a child and how often he got the strap without crying. The child then goes to school next day and hits another child for teasing him, and so on it may go.

In this example, the behaviour 'taking the strap like a man' is reinforced by the father who also models inappropriate (in the eyes of the school) behaviour, setting the stage for a return to the cycle the next day. The strap is a painful but not a punishing stimulus.

'Overcorrection' is a specific application of the punishment by application procedure. It involves requiring subjects to engage repeatedly in the correct behaviour whenever they misbehave or to 'more than make up' for their misbehaviour. An example of the first of these two alternatives is requiring a child who 'forgets' to wash the dishes to do the washing-up for an entire week. An example of the second is requiring an encopretic child to change and wash his or her own clothes and do the rest of the laundry as well.

'Response cost' is another form of punishment. It is defined as the removal of a stimulus such that there is a decreased probability of a behaviour occurring. It is so named because the response costs the person something. A boy hits his brother with a toy and the parent removes the toy from him for the rest of the day. If the removal of the stimulus does not decrease the behaviour in some way, then this is not a response cost.

A popular practice in child care is the use of 'logical consequences'. In most instances, this is merely the concept of response cost with the added provision that the 'cost' be logically connected to the misbehaviour. If a child breaks a window, he must 'pay' for the window in some way. This may be by the removal of money from his bank account, loss of pocket money till the window is paid for or paying the debt by carrying out chores (loss of free time). A child who fails to complete school work within the allotted time may have to stay after school to finish the work (loss of play time). A teenager who uses the telephone for hours on end may lose the privilege for a weekend. These are all 'logical consequences' and examples of response costs.

'Time out' is a specific form of response cost that can be effective in bringing about a reduction in the frequency of a behaviour. The term 'time out' is short for 'time out from available reinforcers'. It involves instituting a period of time following a misbehaviour during which no positive reinforcement is available, regardless of what the person does. This can be achieved by simply ignoring the person and not including him or her in any distribution of reinforcers. More commonly, the person is removed from the situation in some way. A child may be required to sit on a chair in a corner or go to another room while the remaining members of the group continue to engage in enjoyable activities. In extreme cases, when the person refuses to remain in the time out situation and continually intrudes into the group activities or is violent, there may be a need to use 'exclusion time out'. In this case the person is removed to a separate room and confined there for a brief period.

Effective time out is administered in a matter-of-fact manner and usually for brief periods of time:

'John, you seem to be having difficulty being a part of the group today. I think you should take a five-minute break in the corner and we'll see if you're then ready to rejoin the group after that.'

Time out is only effective if the places in which subjects are timed out are less rewarding than those from which they have been removed. Children who hate mathematics may be delighted to be sent out of the classroom. Billy may be having much more fun up in his room with his favourite toys than he would have sitting listening to Great Aunt Martha talk about her string beans.

Time out was commonly used in schools, in business and by parents long before it was 'discovered' by behavioural scientists. How many of us spent time in the corridors outside our classrooms? How many times have we sent our Billys and our Christinas to their rooms? How many union members have been 'sent to Coventry' for cooperating too closely with the management? How many employees and sports figures have been suspended without pay for their misdeeds?

It is important to realise that a stimulus which is an effective reinforcer òr a response cost in one situation, or for one behaviour, may not be so for another. The parents of one child reported that the acquisition of new clothes, particularly dresses, had been a very effective reinforcer for the acquisition and increase of behaviours in the past. But new clothes were ineffective as reinforcers in bringing about an increase in her use of the toilet (she was five years old and a primary encopretic); nor was the removal of her favourite dresses an effective response cost.

While punishment can be quite effective its potential side

effects have often been overlooked. Moreover, its effects may be both time limited and situation specific. Parke (1972) summarised both the factors which help to make punishment more effective and the undesirable side effects that can occur. (See also Craighead, Kazdin and Mahoney, 1981.)

The following factors enhance the suppressive effects of punishment (Craighead *et al.*, 1981):

(1) Immediate application or removal of the contingent stimulus after the undesired response.
(2) Punishment of each and every occurrence of the response.
(3) Introduction of the contingent punishing stimulus at maximal intensity, rather than with gradual increases in severity.

Parke (1972) also notes that, in the case of undesirable behaviours of longer duration, the closer the punishment is to the onset of the response, the more effective the punishment. Likewise, where a misbehaviour is actually a sequence of behaviours, the closer the punishment comes to the start of the sequence, the greater the effect. The relationship of the punishing agent to the subject is also critical. Punishing agents that are perceived as nurturant and affectionate will be more effective than punishing agents who are cold and impersonal. This may be because punishment in this case always involves a response cost – that is, the additional temporary loss of warmth and nurturance. (Obviously this does not apply when punishment is naturalistic and does not involve an interpersonal relationship – such as when we experience pain after touching a hot stove.)

The early behaviourists ignored the importance of thought in the mediation of behaviour, but Parke (1972) showed that a rationale for not performing a behaviour can be an effective suppressor of the behaviour (and hence a punishment even though it may even be pleasant to hear). Thus when children were told a toy was fragile and might break, there was a decrease in rough play with the toy. A rationale also greatly enhances the effectiveness of a punishment that is delivered late and may negate the problem of delayed punishment. The combination of a rationale and punishment (by application or response cost) is the most effective suppressor of behaviour of all. This rationale can include a cognitive re-enactment of the inappropriate behaviour. ('You went into the biscuit tin when I had told you not to and therefore . . .') This can be a potent way of increasing the effect of delayed punishment. Parke (1972) also points out that too intense punishment may interfere with the learning process by raising anxiety to disablingly high levels. This may be a particular problem when the task is to teach a difficult discrimination or a complex task, or to suppress the response to an inappropriate cue or a single wrong behaviour within a difficult chain.

The negative side effects that may arise from punishment include:

- Increased emotional responding.
- Avoidance of the person doing the punishing.
- Imitation of the use of punishment.
- Modelling of aggression.
- Passivity and withdrawal, especially when the punishment is inescapable.
- Decreased quality of relationship with the punishing agent, especially where the frequency of punishment is high, and hence the decreased effectiveness of the punishing agent over time.

Those who have worked with children from abusive homes or with the adult survivors of abusive childhoods know only too well how tragically real these side effects can be.

Other means of reducing problem behaviours

How do we eliminate or reduce problem behaviours if we are to avoid the use of punishment as defined above? Several techniques are available which are not punishment as defined above. The most commonly used is simple problem extinction: identify the event following the behaviour that is the reinforcer and ensure that it no longer occurs following that behaviour.

It is important that when an extinction procedure is used all reinforcing events are eliminated. If they are merely reduced in frequency but still occur, we may well be placing the person on a variable reinforcement schedule and hence *strengthening* the behaviour, not reducing it. Any behaviour which is not reinforced should gradually diminish until it is no longer performed. We need to forewarn the person implementing the extinction procedure (such as a parent or a teacher) that the initial response of the person performing the behaviour will probably be an increase in the behaviour, not a decrease. When a person is expecting a reinforcer and it is not delivered, the first reaction is to try again, work harder to earn the reinforcer or both. Only when it is clear that the reinforcer is no longer available does the behaviour diminish. Verbal mediation of this process, such as informing the child of the new contingencies, may or may not be helpful depending on the child's experience with parents or teachers 'following through' with what they say.

Anyone attempting to use extinction needs also to be aware of the phenomenon of spontaneous recovery. After a behaviour has been successfully reduced to zero by an extinction procedure, it may suddenly start up again for no apparent reason. If it is reinforced again, it will re-establish itself quite quickly. If the extinction contingencies (that is, nonreinforcement) are still in place, it will once again diminish to zero. Often, however, care-givers are caught off guard by this spontaneous recurrence and conclude that the extinction procedure has 'failed'. Extinction and spontaneous recovery make sense if we consider the following hypothetical situation.

A man goes on a gambling holiday for the first time. He enters a casino and tries a slot machine, winning the very first time. He is gleeful and immediately tries the slot machine again and is lucky enough to win again. He puts more coins in the slot machine and wins several more times. We now have a well-established behaviour. However, unbeknown to our novice gambler, his luck has run out and the slot machine stops delivering jackpots. When he has put several more coins in and not received any more winnings he gets perturbed and starts putting coins in more quickly than before (possibly also pulling the lever more vigorously, hitting the machine and swearing under his breath). As the machine continues to accept money without delivering anything in return, his rate of putting coins in the machine slows until he 'gives up'. He may then go on to other slot machines, try roulette and blackjack, trying to regain his 'winning streak' (re-establish the reinforcing contingencies). But our hapless novice's luck has truly run out and he is unsuccessful at all of these other behaviours and machines. Before he goes back home, however, he tries that first machine one more time (spontaneous recovery). If he by chance 'hits the jackpot' again, he may well extend his holiday. If he remains unrewarded he will probably board a plane and consider a different type of holiday next time.

Another nonpunitive method of decreasing an undesirable be-haviour, is to *reinforce an incompatible adaptive behaviour*. We can reward Christine for staying seated rather than punish her for being out of her seat. We can reinforce Juan for sharing his toys rather than punish him for grabbing them back from Nandi. A company can offer bonuses for being on time for work 95 per cent of the time rather than fining or firing for tardiness. We can take the dog for a walk when our spouses ask us nicely rather than yell at them for nagging us. This approach will not work, however, when the existing reinforcement for the behaviour is of greater value than the reinforcement you are offering for the incompatible behaviour. Rewarding a child for working in class is unlikely to be successful if the child derives more benefit from the laughter of his peers as he clowns around. A thank you from a spouse may not be of greater value than a missed 15 minutes of a favourite television sports show.

Two special schedules of reinforcement must be mentioned in any discussion of nonpunitive ways of decreasing unwanted behaviours. They are special because they reward the absence of behaviour, not its presence.

The first of these is the DRO schedule, or Differential Reinforcement of Other behaviour. This is an interval schedule of reinforcement whereby the person is rewarded for not performing a certain behaviour over a specified time period. Again, parents knew of these techniques long before behavioural scientists discovered them. How many of us were told, as children, that we could have a special dessert if we went all day without hitting our brother or sister, or if we didn't have an 'accident' in our pants, or if we stayed out of mud puddles while wearing our Sunday clothes? Being rewarded for not doing something is part of the process of learning self-control. Another example of this schedule was paying farmers *not* to grow certain crops, practised by western governments a few years back.

The other schedule is similar. It is the DRL schedule or Differential Reinforcement of Low rates of behaviour. This is a mixed ratio-interval schedule whereby a person is reinforced whenever the number of times they perform a behaviour within a certain period of time is less than the criterion number. 'You can go out and play with your friends this afternoon Sally, as long as you don't watch more than two cartoons on TV this morning.' 'The company wishes to announce a contest. The employee with the fewest invoice errors this month will receive a gift certificate for $25.00 for Ollie's Restaurant.'

The maximum number of times the behaviour is allowed can gradually be reduced in a step down procedure. This is especially useful for reducing behaviours that occur at a high rate. Some people have 'discovered' this schedule in trying to reduce addictive behaviours. They reward themselves for smoking fewer cigarettes each day or drinking fewer cups of coffee. Parents can use this to reduce gradually the number of times a child gets out of bed before settling at night. This may be less traumatic for the child than procedures requiring an immediate reduction to zero of 'out of bed' episodes.

Multiple targets

So far our emphasis has been on changing single behaviours. But rarely do our clients present with a single, easily definable, focal problem. More often, they present with a variety of problem behaviours. It is possible and sometimes desirable that we tackle each problem behaviour one by one. Sometimes, the order in which behaviours must be dealt with is readily apparent. If we are presented with an anorexic client with recent severe weight loss and a history of underachievement, we must address the lack of food intake first and the school problems second. But if we are presented with a patient who is both self-injurious and danger-ously violent, we can hardly ignore one while addressing the other.

The list of presenting problems can be both long and serious. The patient or the guardian or both may tell you to get lost if you suggest dealing with the problems one at a time and ignoring the other behaviours in the meantime.

One solution is to analyse each of the problem behaviours, develop a plan for each one, and implement them all simultane-ously. This may work for a limited number of presenting prob-lems, if those implementing the treatments are both dedicated and patient. But asking too much of treatment personnel may result in all the programmes being poorly implemented and in-effective. Not only will this result in a lack of effective change, but it may also set up expectations of failure and feelings of inade-quacy in the patient and the treatment staff, and may lead to treatment drop-out.

When there are multiple behaviours to be modified or taught, a useful procedure is to establish a *token economy*. In this, many be-haviours are targeted simultaneously and rewarded with tokens. Tokens are some type of marker that indicates credits earned. These credits can then be exchanged at specified times for back-up reinforcers. Back-up reinforcers are goods, services and privileges that patients pay for with their tokens and that give the tokens their value.

It is also useful to use a token economy when there is a need to ensure fairness among the members of a social group. Siblings or fellow patients may become upset if they perceive that the identified patient's misbehaviour has earned them a special status with unique access to desirable rewards. Placing everyone within a given environment on the same programme ensures fairness.

Another technique that can be used with either single or multiple targets of behaviour is *behavioural contracting*. A behavioural contract is a *negotiated* contract between the patient and the person implementing the programme, whether that be parents, teachers, ward staff, the therapist or someone else. The agreement is written out and signed by all parties involved. The contract specifies who is to perform the behaviour (for example, teenage daughter), the behaviour to be performed (or not to be performed in a DRO contract), the criterion for successful completion (for example, bed must be made five days out of seven with sheets and blankets tucked in, no visible wrinkles and the pillow at the head of the bed), the reward to be given (perhaps use of the car for three hours), when the reward will be given (Friday night) and by whom (parents). Alternatively, this contract might specify several behaviours to be performed, all of which must be done to earn the reward; several behaviours, the completion of any resulting in the reward; or several behaviours each with its own reward to be delivered regardless of the performance or non-performance of the other behaviours.

A distinct advantage of behavioural contracts is that the patients have a significant say in the programmes developed for them. This makes it particularly useful with teenagers who may engage in 'countercontrol behaviour' (the opposite of what is demanded by the programme) when treatment programmes are imposed upon them.

Chapter 5

Cognitions

A girl watches her peers play a complex game she has never seen before. After watching several rounds, she asks to join in and wins the first time she plays. A chimpanzee sits on the floor of his cage and looks at a banana which is suspended from the ceiling but is out of reach. He then looks at a group of boxes placed randomly on the floor of his cage. He suddenly places boxes one on top of another and gets the banana without any trial and error learning (Kohler, 1925). Another primate is taught sign language and generates meaningful new combinations of signs (Gardner and Gardner, 1975). A man is skiing down a resort mountain when he stops and looks at the crisscrossing tracks in the snow. With sudden insight, he solves a problem and wins a Nobel prize for discovering the double helix model of genetic structure (Watson, 1968).

Learning by cognition

What do these four events have in common? They all demonstrate learning without trial and error or shaping. It is learning by cognition, by induction and deduction, by insight. And it points to one of the limitations of traditional learning theories – classical and operant – namely the inability of these theories to explain single-trial learning of sometimes quite complex responses, and the generation of well-planned, successful, novel solutions to problems without trial and error learning.

Learning occurs not only when a person by chance or shaping emits a response and then purposefully or randomly gets rewarded for the behaviour. Both animal and human studies have shown that organisms can acquire new reponses without ever being reinforced (Mischel, 1971). People can arrive at novel solutions through problem solving. They can acquire new behaviours through modelling, mental rehearsal and imagery, and instruction from therapists, parents, teachers and books (why else would you be reading this book?). People can reinforce themselves by establishing their own contingencies, praising themselves and making attributions that result in positive emotional states ('I have a right to feel proud that I am working on this book instead of watching the football match!') Understanding how cognitions aid in the acquisition and maintenance of behaviours adds yet another tool with which the therapist may alter behaviour patterns which present problems.

Further evidence for the power of cognitive variables is provided by the well-documented placebo effect. This effect is a physiological, psychological or psychophysiological reaction to a drug which cannot be attributed to its chemical properties (Shapiro and Morris, 1978). A person's expectation that he or she will improve seems, in some cases, to be all that is needed to bring about 'cures' of pain, headaches, anxiety, colds and a host of other disorders. In a similar vein, many of the behavioural effects attributed to the pharmacological properties of alcohol may be due mainly to the beliefs about the effects of alcohol held by the drinker. While alcohol has well-established physiological actions, various studies have demonstrated that it is the belief that alcohol has been consumed that determines the 'behavioural' response, not the actual consumption (Lang, Goeckner, Adesso and Marlatt, 1975; Pihl, 1983; Murdoch and Pihl, 1988).

The roles of cognitions

Some might question the place of a chapter on cognitions in a *behaviour* therapy text. Only those who view behaviour therapy strictly within an SR model (stimulus-response with no intervening variables) àre likely to do this. In reality, the SR model is extremely hard, if not impossible, to defend as a sufficient model to explain, predict and control behaviour in the light of current evidence for the role of cognitive mediators of behaviour (Craighead, Kazdin and Mahoney, 1981; Dobson, 1988 (Chapter 1); Gardner, 1985).

It is not our intention here to delve into the whole field of cognitive and cognitive-behavioural approaches to human behaviour. Rather, we aim to introduce the concepts and roles cognitions play within a behavioural context. In doing so, we are using the social learning model which states that the organism is an important intervening variable in the SR link: SORC – Stimulus-*Organism*-Response-Consequence.

Bandura and Walters (1963) and Hebb (1966) maintain that learning is facilitated by reinforcement but is not dependent upon it. Learning is regulated by sensory and cognitive processes, as responses are acquired. People do not always use all the behaviours they have learned. It is the *performance* of a behaviour – that is, the likelihood that it will be performed in a certain situation – that seems to be much more determined by operant and classical conditioning factors.

Luria (1961) and Vygotsky (1962) investigated the emergence of verbal control or mediation of behaviour in children. This work contributed greatly to the development of cognitive-behavioural interventions with children (Braswell and Kendall, 1988).

Beck *et al.* (1979, page 3), in their ground-breaking volume on the cognitive therapy of depression, states that cognitive therapy is based on the underlying rationale that

' . . . an individual's affect and behaviour are largely determined by the way in which he structures the world . . . His cognitions (verbal or pictorial "events" in the stream of consciousness) are based on attitudes or assumptions (schemas), developed from previous experiences.'

Beck (1976), among others, notes that this view is not new but has been around since the days of the ancient Greeks. He points out that Epictetus believed that 'men are not moved by things but by the views which they take of them'. The view of most cognitive-behavioural therapists seems to be that cognitions act as mediators affecting the impact the environment has on the subject. The person encounters a situation which is then altered in some way by cognitions before a response is emitted (Craighead, Kazdin and Mahoney, 1981; Dobson, 1988). This altered view of the situation may be very similar to that of others in the situation, resulting in a sense of 'shared reality'. In other cases, the mediating influence of the person's cognitions will result in an idiosyncratic interpretation that sets the person apart from others in that situation. The result will probably be either personal discomfort, interpersonal discomfort or both.

Take, for example, two people who are presented with identical situations: a man asks them to drive him to the airport. One of them reacts with a pleasant 'no'. The other makes a rude, angry remark. Why the difference in the responses to the same request?

Traditional behavioural approaches would simply consider the learning histories of the two people, the probabilities that in similar situations, similar responses would occur and the consequences of the responses. On a practical level, we do not always have access to accurate detailed learning histories of our patients and they, untrained as they are in behavioural analysis, cannot give us such histories. Furthermore, the action may be 'totally out of character', a response that to the best of anyone's recollection is a unique one for that individual.

A different and potentially more productive approach is to investigate how the two people perceived and interpreted the same situation. One way to do this is to ask them what they said to themselves before they responded. The first might have simply said: 'I dislike driving all that way through heavy traffic. I'll only be resentful if I do, so I better say no.' The second person may have said: 'People make me so angry. They are always taking advantage of my good nature, making unreasonable requests and expecting me to agree meekly no matter how much trouble it puts me to – and they rarely say thank you or even offer to pay for the petrol it costs me. Well for once, I'm going to say no and let this inconsiderate oaf know how I feel.'

Thus the same request is interpreted very differently by the two people. One makes an internal attribution about feelings ('I' statements) and the other makes external ('he/she', 'they' statements). One makes an assertive positive self statement ('I better say no') while the other makes an unassertive self statement ('People are always taking advantage of me') and then an aggressive self statement ('. . . let this inconsiderate oaf know how I feel'). It is these internal processes of perception and interpretation, planning and evaluation that are at the core of the cognitive aspects of behaviour therapy.

Memory

There must be some variable that connects prior experience to the current situation, in order to explain experimental results such as the above. Prior learning must be represented and retained in some manner, available at a moment's notice for comparison with the current situation. Clearly, we are talking about memory here. Memory, however, is not a complete, objectively accurate retention of all prior experience.

The channel down which information travels to be stored has a limited capacity. This was eloquently shown in Miller's (1956) article, 'The magical number seven plus or minus two'. He showed that this limitation is overcome by reducing and transforming the information through such processes as 'chunking' or grouping larger sets of information into smaller sets. If asked to remember the numbers 7-5-3 (seven, five, three), for example, we have three pieces of information to remember, but if we say to ourselves 753 (seven hundred and fifty-three) we have only one piece of information to remember. In other words, our brains are not passive recipients of external stimuli from the environment (antecedents and consequences) but active processors of that information. Furthermore, we reduce the information by 'encoding' it in some way, creating a representation of it in our storage systems. The method of encoding is often by the use of language. When we need the information at some future time, we must then 'decode' the stored material to bring it back into a usable format. All of these processes make the brain more efficient at dealing with information, but they also introduce more places where errors in processing the information can occur.

Differential attention

We can back the process up even further. We are constantly bombarded through all our senses with more information than we can process. We actively attend to some things in our environment and actively block out others. In other words, the mediation of cognitive function is not only reactive to environmental influences, it also proactively determines those parts of the environment to which we will give our attention. For example, a phobic person will selectively attend to those aspects of the environment that signal danger, depressed individuals to those aspects of their experience that confirm their feelings of low self-worth.

Our ability to encode, decode and transform information gives us the capacity to create fiction, to invent, to paint scenes we have never seen and to dream of what could be. Imagination, creativity and foresight are only possible because we actively 'create' our own realities rather than directly perceiving reality. It is also our bane, because it is at the core of our capacity to distort those personal realities into experiences of unwarranted pain and suffering through the very same processes.

The evolution of cognitive therapy

The transition from a strictly 'behavioural' behaviour therapy into 'cognitive-behaviour therapy' resulted from the operation of forces both from within the behaviour therapy movement and from outside the frontiers of behaviourism. According to Dobson (1988), six independent factors have each played their part in leading to the widespread acceptance of the cognitive perspective:

(1) The growing recognition by the late 1960s that SR behaviourism was inadequate on its own to account for all of human behaviour. In particular, Bandura's (1969) demonstration that children could learn strictly through observation of a model without themselves experiencing the consequences of the behaviour; the research on delay of gratification (Mischel, Ebsen and Zeiss, 1972); and Vygotsky's (1962) demonstration that children learned grammatical rules that their parents and teachers were unable to discriminate well enough to reinforce selectively, all pointed inescapably to the role of mediating factors.

(2) The founders of cognitive therapy continued to reject traditional psychoanalytic therapies at the same time as they were becoming dissatisfied with strictly SR, nonmediational model. They questioned the efficacy of psychodynamic therapies which, they believed, lacked empirical evidence of effectiveness.

(3) A rigid adherence to observable behaviours as targets of therapy narrowed the range of therapy and left significant aspects of disorders untreated, for example, the obsessive thoughts of patients in cases in which only the compulsive actions were treated.

(4) Advances in cognitive psychology, particularly the development of information-processing models of cognitions, provided a framework for understanding how mediational concepts could work.

(5) The emergence of therapists and theorists who labelled themselves cognitive-behaviourists drew attention to the field and its ideas.

(6) Empirical proof, in the shape of outcome studies, demonstrated the efficacy of cognitive approaches.

Basic premises

Cognitive approaches to therapy have three premises in common. These are:

(1) Cognitive activity affects behaviour.
(2) Cognitive activity may be monitored and altered.

(3) Desired behaviour change may be effected through cognitive change (Dobson, 1988, page 4).

Dobson considers the evidence for the first assumption to be overwhelming, as do others (Gardner, 1985; Beck, Rush, Shaw and Emery, 1979; Craighead, Kazdin and Mahoney, 1981). The evidence for the second premise is still the subject of empirical research but there are reliable and valid self-report instruments available that help to identify cognitive errors. (See Corcoran and Fisher, 1987.) There is also growing evidence for the effectiveness of the cognitive approaches to therapy (Beck, 1987; Craighead, Kazdin and Mahoney, 1981). However, it is harder to establish that it is specifically the changes in cognitions that account for the results (Dobson, 1988).

The roles cognitions play

Cognitions cannot be conveniently slotted into behavioural sequences since they function at almost every step. They are stimuli like any others and can even be considered behaviours themselves. (Remember our three-dimensional view of behaviour – motor, physiological and *cognitive-emotional*.) Consider the following observed sequence: a parent asks a child to take out the rubbish, the child says yes and then continues to watch television, whereupon the parent yells at the child who yells back.

From a strict behavioural point of view, we might describe the sequence as:

Antecedent: Request.
Behaviour: Verbal agreement but motor noncompliance.
Consequence: Yell.
Behaviour: Yell.

Limited to this information, we are likely to decide that we have a noncompliant child and set up programmes to increase the child's compliance. However, let us add some cognitions that might also have occurred at the same time:

Parent requests child to take out the rubbish.

Child says yes and thinks: 'I'll do it as soon as this show is over.'

Parent notices child doesn't move and thinks: 'There goes that child again, not respecting me, challenging me, not listening, well we'll see who's boss around here.'

Parent then yells.

Child thinks: 'What have I done now, I said I'd do it, they're never satisfied, why should I even try, I'm so angry!'

Child then yells.

Now we can see the possibility of intervening cognitively by suggesting to the parent that the child is not disrespectful, once the cognitions are taken into account. The child had every intention of carrying out the behaviour the parent desired. In this case, as we can now see, it was not the behaviour of the child that elicited the parent's behaviour but rather the attributions that the parent made about that behaviour.

Chapter 6

Cognitions: Basic Concepts

Cognitive processes can be maladaptive in various ways. Thinking can be erroneous. It can be erroneous in content because of inaccurate premises (such as dysfunctional beliefs) or because of inaccurate perceptions and attributions (as, for example, in paranoid ideation). It can also be erroneous in process (errors in logic and thinking style), as in 'catastrophising'.

Deficits in cognitive skills can also be the basis of clients' difficulties. Those with deficient problem-solving skills may act in inappropriate ways because they do not consider all the alternatives open to them. Impulsive individuals may be impulsive because they have never acquired the skill of stopping and considering the consequences of their actions. Kendall and Braswell (1985) have developed an entire treatment programme that addresses the problem of impulsive behaviour in children, based on this idea. One has only to look at the profound impact of severe cognitive deficits such as mental retardation, illiteracy and aphasia to appreciate the dramatic impact cognitive deficits can have on human behaviour.

The things we say to ourselves and our internal images serve many functions. They mediate between a stimulus and a response, including the emotional reaction we have to an event. They can be viewed as antecedents and as consequences and as behaviours in themselves.

Our thoughts can be mediators between the objective events around us, our subjective reaction and our motor responses. Consider two children in a school playground. Both wear glasses. Both are called 'four eyes' by the other children. One smiles, the other frowns and walks away. The difference may be in the interpretation each gives to the term 'four eyes'. Perhaps our smiling child says to herself: 'They've given me a nickname, so that means I'm accepted.' The other child may say to himself: 'They called me a name. That means they don't like me.'

The words and images in our stream of consciousness can

function as antecedents as well. The thought 'Is the stove turned off?' or the image of one's house burning may cause one to turn the car around and double check the controls on the stove. Remembering or imagining past hurts or imagining infidelity may trigger an angry outburst in a spouse – one that leaves others wondering what is the matter.

Our internal dialogue can be considered a behaviour in its own right and a specific target of change, not just a mediator of behaviour change. We need look no further than the repetitive, intrusive thoughts of some sufferers from obsessive-compulsive disorders to see this. Or a man may never have engaged in sexual behaviour with children, but every time he sees a young girl in a dress he is distressed by sexual thoughts and images concerning the girl. This is no less a response than any motor action would be.

Finally, our self-talk can be one of the consequences of our behaviour. We reward and punish our actions with the things we say to ourselves. We can tell ourselves we did a good job. Or we can belittle our efforts. These comments may or may not have any objective basis and can enhance, diminish or have little relation to externally imposed rewards such as the comments of others. To a comment such as 'You gave a good talk today', the subject might say to herself 'She's right, I did do well'; or 'How can she say that, the talk was lousy?'; or 'I don't care much about her opinion, I think it was/wasn't a good talk.'

The following sequences of events provide examples of the many faces of cognitions:

(1) Antecedent: Mother asks child to take out the rubbish.
(2) Cognition (response to (1)/antecedent to (3)): Child thinks: 'There she goes again, picking on me. Not this time!'
(3) Child makes overt response which is the second behaviour in a behavioural chain, the first being the cognition in (2): 'No!'
(4) Child has a cognition which is the third in the chain and also a reward for behaviour in (3): (To self) 'I showed her!'

Or consider a child engaged in a self-instructional sequence (which will be explained more fully later in this chapter):

(1) Antecedent thoughts: 'I have to remember the steps the therapist taught me. First I have to look at the problem carefully and see what I have to do.'
(2) Behaviour: 'The problem is to add these two numbers, then subtract this one.'

(3) Consequence (reward): 'So far, so good. I'm doing well.'
(4) Antecedent thought: 'What do I have to do next? I have to go slow and finish the whole problem without jumping ahead.'
(5) Behaviour: 'Now I have to divide by two and then multiply by seven. I'll just whip through this. It's so easy.'
(6) Consequence (punishment): 'Oh no, I got it wrong. Oh, I was supposed to divide by seven and multiply by two. I have to go slower next time and read the problem more carefully'.

Assessment of cognitions

Patients (and people in general) are not always aware of their internal dialogues (Beck *et al.*, 1979). Rather, they frequently act in a 'mindless' manner, as if they were following a script, except when they are forced to make a choice or a judgment such as might happen in a novel situation (Meichenbaum, 1985).

'Automatic thoughts' are frequently referred to by cognitive-behaviour therapists. These are the thoughts that occur without apparent volition. They are frequently very rapid (Beck, 1976). They usually occur in parallel with more volitional thought processes and frequently are of an evaluative nature. Some patients are well aware of this parallel train of ideation but others need to practise to become aware of the stream of parallel thought. It is these thoughts which seem to precede and trigger emotional states. Meichenbaum (1985) likens them to overlearned behaviours, in that they are activated in a similar way to habitual behaviours, without conscious volition. When we drive a car in a routine situation or perform any well-learned behaviour, we are rarely aware of the thought processes involved. Our automatic thoughts are very similar (Meichenbaum, 1985).

Beck (1976) tells us that the role of automatic thoughts was suggested to him when he was practising psychoanalysis, by the report of a patient. This patient reported two streams of thought. The first comprised the thoughts that occurred to him as he free associated in the manner taught to subjects in psychoanalysis. The second consisted of self-critical comments and his affect at the time was more related to this second stream. When Beck asked other patients to report this second stream of thought, some were readily able to do so while others could do so only with considerable effort and by selectively attending to these thoughts. This suggests that the self-monitoring of one's thoughts is important.

Such self-monitoring can be promoted by instructing patients in the nature of automatic thoughts and having them attend to this other stream of consciousness. This is usually done by teaching them the 'ABC' technique (Ellis and Harper, 1975). Patients are asked to 'fill in the blanks' with the automatic thoughts which represent the 'Belief' that comprises the connection between the 'Activating stimulus' and the 'Conditioned response'. In the shortform we have been using, it is the client helping to put the 'O' between the 'S' and the 'R' of SORC. Meichenbaum (1985) describes a variety of techniques for self-monitoring that can be tailored to the specific problems being addressed.

The assessment of cognitions need not rely on self-monitoring alone. Segal and Shaw (1988), reviewing the issues and techniques of cognitive assessment, note that there are three domains and seven categories of cognitions that may need to be assessed in a problem situation. The domains, also referred to as levels of cognitive analysis, are:

- Cognitive structures.
- Processes.
- Products.

The categories which cut across all three levels of analysis are:

- Imagery.
- Attributions.
- Beliefs.
- Self-efficacy expectations.
- Cognitive style.
- Self statements.
- *In vivo* thought sampling.

The assessment techniques can include:

- Clients 'thinking aloud' as they complete tasks.
- Clients writing down or recording spontaneous private speech.
- Self-monitoring by random sampling (at randomly selected points in time – 'What are you thinking about right now?').
- Incident-related self-monitoring ('When the problem occurs, write down your thoughts').
- Videotaped thought reconstruction, in which a patient views

a videotape of a real or role-played situation and recalls the thoughts which occurred at the time.
- Questionnaires which list thoughts and ask those completing them to endorse which thoughts are most like the thoughts that would occur to them.
- A clinical interview in which patients are asked to recall what they were thinking when particular incidents were occurring.

Let us look now at some of these concepts in greater detail.

Attributions

Attributions are the meanings people attach to events – meanings which are not inherent aspects of the events. They often have to do with causation and intent. ('She did/didn't want to hurt my feelings because she is/isn't a mean person.') The importance of attibutions is nowhere more evident than in our criminal justice system, in which the seriousness of a crime and the subsequent consequences ride on attributions. If a person kills another person intentionally (an attribution) we deal with that person more harshly than if we attribute the death to misadventure or care-lessness rather than intent. When we analyse a patient's cogni-tions, consideration of that person's attributions is crucial. Attributions are important both in themselves and because they help point to irrational beliefs the person may hold (see below).

Attributions have several relevant dimensions:

Dimension 1
This is concerned with *internal* versus *external* attribution of causation. People can attribute the cause of any behaviour either to themselves or to people or events external to themselves. This can have important ramifications. Neither style of attribution is inherently good or bad. At times psychological health seems to be enhanced by internal attributions; at other times external attribu-tions seem more helpful.

People whose self-esteem is high generally attribute pleasant consequences to internal factors ('He likes me because I treated him well'); and unpleasant or undesirable events to external factors ('She didn't like me because she was having a bad day'). On the other hand, those whose self-esteem is poor tend to make attributions of external or even chance causation for happy events ('I got a rise because the boss was in a good mood, not because I deserved it'); and internal attributions of cause for unpleasant events ('I didn't get the rise because I'm a rotten employee') (Pope, McHale and Craighead, 1988). It is not surprising that Beck *et al.* (1979) have identified the same tendency in patients who are depressed, given the close relationship between low self-esteem and depression.

Dimension 2

This is concerned with whether the cause of the difficulty is perceived as *stable* or *unstable*. Once again, neither is inherently associated with positive mental health. The context is important, as it is with Dimension 1. Healthy mental states are associated with attributions of stable causes for pleasant events and unstable causes for unpleasant events. Psychological discomfort and mal-adaptive behaviour tend to be associated with the reverse attributions (Pope *et al.*, 1988). Thus students who obtain good marks in examinations may attribute their success to the fact that they are of high intelligence (a stable characteristic) and feel good about themselves. Other students may attribute their success to luck (which is likely to be unstable). For example, they may believe that the exam papers were marked in a hurry so that many mistakes were missed and they will probably 'get caught' next time.

Emotionally healthy individuals tend to attribute 'negative' emotions to unstable events. So the student who gets a 'D' may say to herself: 'I had a bad week when I did that essay, I can do better next time', implying that her poor performance was due to an unstable and changeable set of circumstances. A less adaptive response would be to attribute it to stable, unchangeable factors; such a student might say to herself: 'I'm really stupid. I finally got the mark I deserve. I don't know how I managed to fool them all the other times'.

Dimension 3

Attributions may be *global* or *specific*. That is to say, events may be perceived as due to generalized factors that exist in many situations or to factors which are specific to the particular case.

A student getting an 'A' in a term paper may make the global attribution that this was because he is a good student or the specific attribution that he is good only at short stories. Depression and other generally undesirable clusters of emotional/behavioural characteristics tend to be associated with the attribution of global causes to negative events and specific causes to pleasant events. ('The boss fired me because I'm a rotten employee and I always have been'; or 'I probably wasn't laid off with everyone else because of a clerical error'.) The reverse is true of emotionally healthy individuals.

Attributions and interpersonal relationships

Attributions play a role not only in mood states and related behaviours but also in interpersonal relationships. This is because we can apply the same dimensions of attribution to others as we can to ourselves. Compare 'We're fighting because he's always been a real creep (stable-global-external to speaker, internal to spouse)' with 'We're fighting because this home renovation is taking so long (unstable-specific-external)'.

A marriage counsellor is likely to achieve success more quickly with a couple sharing the second set of attributions than in the situation in which one or both of the partners make the first set of attributions. Indeed studies have shown that members of distressed marriages tend to make global, stable, negative attributions about each other, whereas they attribute their partner's positive behaviours to unstable, specific factors (Epstein, Schlesinger and Dryden, 1988). Our own experience with families in distress over the behaviour of their children is that they also make similar negative-global-stable-internal attributions about the problem child and that therapy is unlikely to proceed well without a shift in such attributions.

Expectations

Closely related to attributions are the subject's expectations. Expectations may even arise from an attribution. ('I'm really stupid (internal-stable-global attribution) so it is only a matter of time before the supervisor finds out and fires me (expectancy).') Frequently, we see people act not in response to what actually preceded their behaviour but what they expected to occur. A good example of this occurred in my (Douglas Murdoch's) undergraduate days. I was quite preoccupied one day as I was selecting a meal in the cafeteria, when I met an acquaintance. He said, 'Hello, how are you?' and even though what he said registered at some level, I didn't answer because of my preoccupation. However, he carried blithely along and said, 'Oh, I'm fine thank you,' at exactly the right interval of time as if I had replied. When I checked with him afterwards, he said he didn't realise I hadn't answered him, so strong was his expectation of a reply.

The problem presented by expectations is well illustrated in various psychiatric disorders, but perhaps in none more strikingly than in the case of paranoid personality disorders. Patients with such disorders have so marked an expectation of rejection and hostility that neutral events are regularly interpreted as hostile acts. The power of these particular cognitions – namely, the expectations that the acts of others will be hostile – is well shown by the resistance to change usually displayed by these subjects. The subject's paranoid attributions often lead to the misinterpretation of the interventions of the therapist as well.

The expectations involved in other problems may be less obvious. 'Conditional probabilities' are a class of expectations that need attention in many cases. They are the estimated probabilities that an event will occur. They are something which we constantly consider when thinking about our behavioural options. Take the example of driving to an appointment for which you will be late if you obey the speed limit. Will you exceed the speed limit in order to get to the meeting on time? In the brief time that it will take you to make your decision, you have probably considered many conditional probabilities. 'What are the chances the police will be on this route?'; 'What are the chances of an accident on this road if I speed?'; and 'What is the chance of a serious consequence if I'm late for the meeting?'

Many patients have conditional expectancies that are extreme in some way. People who are phobic have the expectation that there is an unrealistically high probability that a feared event (such as plane crash) will occur. Beck (1976) considers this a core feature distinguishing phobias from fears. A change in the estimated probability of being victimised is a documented effect in many victims of crime (Himelein, 1989; Veronen, 1989).

Self-efficacy

A person's self-efficacy consists of the specific beliefs the person holds about his or her ability to perform a task or a class of tasks. We are referring here to people's beliefs in their *ability* to perform behaviours, not to their beliefs concerning the outcomes of the behaviours. One can expect a good outcome but still not engage in a behaviour because one does not expect to be able to execute the behaviour with a sufficient degree of skill. I am sitting here (wondering if I have the skill to complete this book!) in part because 12 years ago I did not believe that I would ever run the 100 metre sprint fast enough to compete in the Olympics, even though that was a desirable goal for me. This concept was first put forward by Bandura (1969) and has been the subject of extensive research since then. It has also been widely used by behaviour therapists.

Errors in information processing

It is important to distinguish realistic thoughts and perceptions from distorted ones. The probability of being a victim of crime will vary depending on where a person lives. For some, it is realistic and prudent to be fearful of going out alone after dark. But it is also clear that some people's thinking leads to distortions in the way they perceive themselves, their world and their future. How do these distortions arise? Beck *et al.* (1979, page 14) identified a number of cognitive errors or 'faulty information processing' that lead to the distortions. These are:

(1) *Arbitrary inference* (a response set). This refers to the process of drawing a conclusion in the absence of evidence to support that conclusion, or when the evidence points to the contrary conclusion.

(2) *Selective abstraction* (a stimulus set). This consists of focussing on detail taken out of context, ignoring other more salient features of the situation and conceptualising the whole experience on the basis of this fragment.

(3) *Overgeneralisation* (a response set). This refers to the pattern of drawing a general rule or conclusion on the basis of one or more isolated incidents, and applying the concept across the board to related and unrelated situations.

(4) *Magnifying or minimising* (response sets). These are cognitive errors in evaluating the significance or magnitude of events that are so gross as to constitute distortions.

(5) *Personalisation* (a response set). This refers to people's proclivities to relate external events to themselves when there is no basis for making such connections.

(6) *Absolutist, dichotomous thinking* (a response set). This is manifested in the tendency to place all experiences in one of

two opposite categories, for example, flawless or defective, immaculate or filthy, saint or sinner.

Cognitive styles: schemas and beliefs

The cognitive styles of all of us are subject to error from time to time, but depressed patients differ in that cognitive errors are characteristic of their way of processing information about themselves and their world. These can be organised into enduring rules of knowing that become schemas, or a set of organised rules for perceiving and understanding events. In the case of depressed patients, these schemas involve information processing rules that ensure that the persons they have contact with, and the events that occur around them, will be perceived negatively (Beck *et al.*, 1979). In the case of an agoraphobic person, a schema has developed consisting of seeing events, objects and people as dangerous in some way.

The amount of information that our brains are bombarded with at any moment is more than we can process. Thus our brains must select and deal with the most relevant information and exclude all other information. This leads to the phenomenon of selective perception. We are selective in what we attend to and process. We exhibit a wide range of individual differences in this regard. The schemas just referred to help determine what information will be attended to and what information will be 'filtered out'.

Consider a family drive in the country, the driver being a teenager who has just obtained her provisional licence. The girl may be attending very closely to all the new information and sensations related to driving and selectively attending to her own feelings of accomplishment. The father may be selectively attending to the minor (or not so minor!) deviations from the car's intended line of travel, and to thoughts about the car being less than a year old and the increased cost of insurance should they have an accident. The brother may be selectively attending to the lack of eligible girls in the car at that moment or in the immediate vicinity and to memories of all the times his sister has been favoured over him. The mother may be selectively attending to her husband's rapid and frequent admonishments to the daughter to be careful and watch out for that oncoming car (that at the moment is a dot on the horizon), and to thoughts about how he is always picking on the daughter and would never be so nervous and cautioning to their son.

Beck *et al.* (1979) has described a *cognitive triad*, in an attempt to elaborate further the role of these faulty schemas in depression. He considers that they occur within three domains which make up the triad. These are three groups of beliefs about the self:

(1) The depressive schema of the patient (let us assume it is a man) leads him to interpret information and perceptions of himself in a self-derogatory manner. 'He sees himself as defective, inadequate, diseased or deprived. He tends to attribute his unpleasant experiences to a psychological, moral or physical defect in himself . . . because of his presumed defects he is undesirable and worthless.'

(2) The second domain of the cognitive triad is the patient's beliefs about his experience and what these tell him about the world around him. The depressive cognitive schema results in negative interpretations of events so that he sees the world as hostile, rejecting, uncaring or, alternatively, too good for him, too demanding for his 'limited abilities'.

(3) The third aspect of the triad comprises the patient's beliefs about the future. The depressed person's view of the future is that all the negative aspects of himself and his world will be stable and enduring indefinitely. 'He expects unremitting hardship, frustration, and deprivation. When he considers undertaking a specific task in the immediate future, he expects to fail' (Beck *et al.*, 1979, page 11).

Albert Ellis is another pioneer of cognitive therapy. He has developed an approach to therapy known as rational emotive therapy or, in its short form, RET. One of the central aspects of Ellis' approach is the premise that many of us hold beliefs that are irrational and lead to unnecessary anxiety and the associated behaviours. These beliefs bear some resemblance to the schema of Beck's approach. Ellis (1962) identified eleven of these beliefs and refers to them frequently in his writings. They are:

(1) It is essential that a person be loved or approved of by virtually everyone in the community.

(2) A person must be perfectly competent, adequate and achieving to be considered worthwhile.

(3) Some people are bad, wicked or villainous and therefore should be blamed or punished.
(4) It is a terrible catastrophe when things are not as a person wants them to be.
(5) Unhappiness is caused by outside circumstances and a person has no control over it.
(6) Dangerous or fearsome things are cause for great concern and their possibility must be dwelt on continually.
(7) It is easier to avoid certain difficulties and self responsibilities than to face them.
(8) A person should be dependent on others and should have someone stronger on whom to rely.
(9) Past experiences and events are the determinants of present behaviour; the influences of the past cannot be eradicated.
(10) A person should be quite upset over other people's problems and disturbances.
(11) There is always a right or perfect solution to every problem and it must be found or the results will be catastrophic.

It is beyond the scope of this text to elaborate upon these beliefs except to describe briefly how they are used in treatment by an RET therapist. While we all have these beliefs to a greater or lesser extent, because they are basic beliefs of our society, when they become overvalued or indoctrinated through continuous reinforcement they lead to emotional disturbance due to the person's inability to live up to all the 'shoulds', 'oughts' and 'musts'.

The goal of the therapy is to reduce irrational beliefs and replace them with rational ones. This will result in a minimum of self-blame (anxiety, depression) and a minimum of blaming others or circumstances (anger and hostility) (Patterson, 1986). This is accomplished in three stages. The first is to get the patient to recognise the irrational nature of the thoughts and beliefs and how these are connected to the associated uncomfortable feelings and reactions.

The next step is to get the patient to realise that he or she perpetuates the irrational beliefs themselves by continuing to think them and that events in the past cannot be blamed for current modes of thinking. The patient must therefore give up the irrational thoughts and replace them with rational ones.

Finally, therapy moves in the third stage to a wider range of beliefs than those specifically maintaining the difficulty for which the patient has been receiving therapy. There is a broader general discussion of the effects of irrational beliefs. The aim of this is to protect the subject from future difficulties with irrational beliefs not addressed previously in therapy.

Imagery

Cognitions are not confined to self-talk, that is, language. We also think in images. It is important to assess and monitor the imagery clients use as well as images they don't use but could benefit from using (Lazarus, 1984).

Lazarus found that his clients could successfully engage in positive self-talk but still experience negative affect and maladaptive behaviour because the problem situations evoked negative imagery. Furthermore, systematic desensitisation, which uses imagery, is a very successful procedure in many clinical situations. Imagery is often employed in the teaching of relaxation skills. Practising mastery skills such as assertiveness in imagination can also facilitate the acquisition of such skills.

Cognitive errors occur not only because of distorted or erroneous information processing. They can also occur because the information is not fully processed. This can happen as a result of the patient being deficient in some area of thinking. Some of the most commonly encountered deficits are in the areas of attention, impulse control and problem solving. Therapeutic approaches which attempt to teach the skill of using thinking to control one's own behaviour have been developed. First we will look at self-instructional therapy and then at problem solving therapies.

Self-instructional therapy

If we stop and reflect on the interaction of our thinking and our behaviour, we become aware that we seem to regulate our behaviour with our internal dialogue and imagery. We monitor our own behaviour and the reactions of others to our behaviour. We talk ourselves through problems, giving ourselves instructions on the steps we need to take. We might say: 'What seems to be wrong here? This sentence doesn't sound right. Slow down and think now. How else could I write this idea? Would this concept be better presented as a diagram or a chart? Okay, I've got seven or eight ways I can present this idea. What are the pros and cons of each one? I think this is best. No! It still doesn't sound right! This is frustrating! Calm down, if you keep trying you'll get it. Maybe my style reference books will have something. Aha, I see what's wrong. Great! I'm glad I stuck with it and figured it out. Now I know how to get rid of that problem in the future as well.'

This type of internal instruction is common and helpful. However, we do not all use this sort of internal dialogue and the self-instructional approach to regulate our behaviour. The failure to develop the verbal and imagery-mediated self-regulation of behaviour may be a central feature of some disorders. Meichenbaum (1977) noted a lack of internally mediated regulation of behaviour in at least two populations – schizophrenics and impulsive children – and developed self-instructional training to try to teach the skills.

Five steps are taught to these patients. First, they are taught to restate to themselves the requirements of their tasks. They then instruct themselves to perform the tasks slowly and to think before acting. Next, they develop cognitive strategies for dealing with their tasks and imagine themselves carrying out the plans. The patients then make self-reward statements if they have been successful. If they are not successful, they proceed to make self-statements about how to cope with frustration and failure, followed by statements as to what was inappropriate about the solution they came up with and how to correct it.

One of the assumptions of this approach is that the underlying requisite skills (for example, mathematical or conversational skills) are present. All the self-instructional training in the world won't help a child who doesn't know how to perform a particular mathematics problem. It will, however, help the child who makes careless errors, or misses part of the problem, or jumps to conclusions.

Problem solving

Closely related is the area of problem solving. It has been found that some patients seen by mental health professionals have poor problem-solving skills. When confronted with a problem, they have difficulty generating solutions, even when all other indications are that they have average or better than average intelligence. Indeed, the correlation between traditional measures of intelligence and social problem-solving ability is quite low. This may be because the assessment instruments traditionally used to measure intelligence do not measure the ability to think divergently, a cognitive skill related to creativity and social problem solving (D'Zurilla, 1988). We should note, though, that people who score low on measures of intelligence usually score low also on measures on divergent thinking; whereas people who have high scores on intelligence tests may or may not have high scores on divergent thinking (Guilford, 1977). This has led to the analysis of problem solving and to the explicit training of patients in the steps involved in problem solving.

The literature contains many examples of therapies which aim to develop patients' problem-solving skills. Two of the more common ones are 'problem-solving therapy', developed by D'Zurilla and his colleagues (D'Zurilla, 1988) and Mahoney's (1977) 'Personal SCIENCE'.

D'Zurilla (1988) calls these approaches 'prescriptive problem solving'. They are prescriptive in that they designate the manner in which people should solve problems in order to be as successful as possible, rather than descriptive of how people usually solve problems.

The aim of both therapies is for clients to acquire a systematic approach to problem solving. Clients are taught a stepwise procedure for solving problems. This is then applied to the presenting problems. D'Zurilla's (1988) approach involves 20 substeps spread over five major areas.

The five areas involved in problem solving are:

A: Problem information.
B: Emotions.
C: Alternative solutions considered.
D: Solution choice.
E: Solution implementation and outcome.

Mahoney (1977) has framed the problem-solving process in a way which leads to a useful mnemonic. He describes the process as the 'Personal SCIENCE' model because the process is similar to how a scientist approaches a problem and because the first letter of each step forms the word SCIENCE as illustrated below:

S: Specify general problem area.
C: Collect data.
I: Identify patterns or sources.
E: Examine options.
N: Narrow and experiment.

C: Compare data.
E: Extend, revise and replace.

It is worthwhile once again to make the distinction between ability and performance. People may fail to use adequate problem-solving skills either because they do not have them or because they fail to use skills they possess, for any of a number of reasons. Emotional factors will often play a role. D'Zurilla (1988) notes that emotional factors can both facilitate and inhibit problem-solving efforts. A person's general cognitive schemata and approach to problems will also be factors that may need to be addressed before or simultaneously with training in problem-solving skills.

Learning theories are not mutually exclusive

Cognitive, classical conditioning and operant modes of learning have been presented separately with the aim of achieving clarity of presentation, and in order to look at the role of each independently. However, this does not mean that these different modalities of learning operate independently. There is a constant interaction of the cognitive and the more 'traditional' modalities of learning. Meichenbaum (1977) reported that impulsive children's behaviour was not modified by operant reinforcers because they attributed receiving them to luck. But when the children were trained in self-instruction their attributions changed and they were able to benefit from the reinforcement. The recognition of the benefit of instructions on the speed of acquisition of new ways of acting, and the interplay of cognitive, classical and operant modes of learning, is reflected in many of the treatment programmes published in the last few years (for example, Beck *et al.* 1979; Beck and Emery, 1985; Kendall and Braswell, 1985; Meichenbaum, 1985; Pope *et al.*, 1988).

Chapter 7

Behavioural Formulation

If behaviour is learned and maintained according to the rules of learning theory, then each individual will present with a unique configuration of behaviours. This must be the case since no two persons' learning histories are identical. Each has occupied a unique positions in time and space and each person's unique pattern of antecedent stimuli and consequences has had unique results. This means that we must make a unique formulation for each client.

While two people may present to the therapist with behaviours that on the surface are quite similar, for example, the avoidance of interactions with the opposite sex, the underlying circumstances may be very different. A man may avoid women because his mother has subtly but systematically reinforced him every time he has stayed at home with her and punished him each time he has so much as talked about women (operant learning). A different scenario exists in the case of a woman who has had traumatic experiences with men (embarrassment, ridicule) and now has a fear reaction whenever she finds herself in a social situation with men (respondent conditioning). The learning processes involved in the acquisition and maintenance of the avoidant behaviours are different in these two instances. Therefore different approaches to remediation are required.

In the first case, a change in the reinforcement contingencies is necessary, and in the second, an extinction of the fear reaction. It is for such reasons that many behaviourally orientated authors concentrate on what is termed a 'functional analysis of behaviour'.

A functional analysis of behaviour is just what it sounds like: an analysis of the behaviour to determine its function. It involves determining the stimuli which elicit the behaviour, if the behaviour has been classically conditioned, or the reinforcement contingencies maintaining the behaviour and the stimuli which indicate the availability of the reinforcer, if the behaviour is maintained by operant conditioning. This is the assessment phase in behaviour therapy referred to earlier and well described in the article by Kanfer and Saslow (1969). In this endeavour, the goal is not to classify behaviour but to develop an understanding of the unique factors maintaining each client's behaviour. There are specific steps involved that are analogous to conducting a scientific experiment. These are described in the next chapter.

Another approach that has been advocated is to make a diagnosis based on the actions necessary to correct the problem behaviour. This fits more closely the functional purpose of the diagnostic process. It classifies clients' difficulties according to the factors which maintain behaviours (and therefore the actions that are necessary to produce more adaptive functioning), rather than by the appearance of the behaviour problems. It is really the endpoint of a functional analysis of behaviour.

Key concepts

In order to use this latter approach we must understand certain key concepts. These are: *behavioural excess, skill deficit, behavioural deficit* and *behavioural conflict*.

When there is behavioural excess, the operations required are those that reduce the frequency, intensity or duration of a behaviour. In the case of a skill deficit, the operations required are those that will help the person acquire new responses. When there is a behavioural deficit, the operations needed are those that will help the client increase the frequency, duration or intensity of behaviours that are within his or her repertoire but are occurring at a level less than that which is desired. 'Behavioural conflict' refers to the motivational conflict which occurs when a person is faced with two or more mutually exclusive goals.

Behavioural excess

Of all the problems brought to clinicians, more are probably due to behavioural excesses than to any of the other three categories. This applies especially to children's problems. The essence of these problems is the performance of behaviours at rates, intensity levels or durations (or some combination of these) that cause distress to the subject or to others.

The behaviour may have positive or negative connotations.

The critical aspect is that it occurs in excess. Some examples of behavioural excesses are: excessive drinking, handwashing, certain sexual behaviours, aggression, talking, exhibitionism and firesetting, but the list could be extended indefinitely.

Consider the example of excessive consumption of alcohol. A man may present with physical deterioration due to excessive frequency of drinking (several drinks a day), but little drunkenness. Or a woman might present with an excessive intensity of drinking. She may only drink two or three times a year but when she does, she drinks rapidly until she passes out. Or the duration of the drinking may be critical. The client drinks rarely but always goes on ten-day benders that impair all other functioning. A client may also present with drinking that is excessive on two or more of these dimensions. There may be binges, the binges may be frequent and they may almost always end in blackouts.

The mere presence of an excessive behaviour is not enough to classify the problem under the rubric 'behavioural excess'. This is because a behavioural excess may be due to a skill deficit. For example, excessive drinking may be secondary to a deficit in problem-solving skills or stress-management skills – or both. In such cases it is better regarded as an attempt at coping through self-medication.

In other cases, excessive drinking is found to be due to factors which may fit a 'behavioural excess' model. Examples are an 'addictive' situation in which drinking is reinforced through the alleviation of withdrawal symptoms, and a 'social reinforcement' model in which excessive drinking is considered masculine or 'cool' and heavily reinforced within the subject's subculture.

It is because of the above considerations that we need to make a good functional analysis of any behaviour we wish to modify. It is only when we know the function of the behaviour, the conditions under which it occurs and the consequences maintaining it, that we can determine the most effective course of action.

When a behaviour fits the diagnostic category of behavioural excess, techniques which will reduce the features of the behaviour that are in excess – frequency, intensity and/or duration – are indicated. These techniques include: reinforcement of incompatible responses, reinforcement of low rates of behaviour (DRL), reinforcement of the absence of the behaviour (DRO), removal of the reinforcement contingencies (extinction), pairing either the behaviour or the stimuli associated with the behaviour (or both) with an agent which evokes an undesirable reflex response (such as the use of disulphuram which induces nausea when alcohol is drunk) or – less to be desired – the use of one of the punishment paradigms (see Chapter 4).

Skill deficits

A skill deficit exists when a person lacks the ability which is necessary to perform a needed behaviour. A performance deficit, on the other hand, exists when a person can perform the necessary behaviour but fails to do so when required.

Let us take the example of a girl presenting with failure to complete mathematics tasks. She has a skill deficit if she lacks the ability to complete the tasks. This might have resulted from a lack of learning opportunities, poor instructional methods, a learning disability or an unduly short attention span. She has a performance deficit if she fails to complete the tasks but can demonstrate the ability to do the work of which they consist – or has in the past demonstrated such ability and has suffered no disease or injury which might explain loss of the ability (for example, injury to the brain).

This may seem a simple distinction but in practice it is often difficult to make. Nevertheless, it is frequently a key distinction if an effective intervention plan is to be developed. This is especially true when we are dealing with children, since children with skill deficits often present with behaviour that resembles that of children with performance deficits. A child with a skill deficit may present with the same avoidance, distractibility, aggression and anger as a child who has the necessary mathematical skills but whose behaviour problems interfere with their use. Sometimes, the child is well aware of the underlying problem, and prefers being seen as having a behaviour problem to being seen as 'stupid'.

Establishing that we are dealing with a child with a performance deficit – that is, one who can perform the skill under different conditions or has demonstrated the behaviour in the past – can be difficult. It is not enough to have significant others declare that they 'know' the child can do the work but simply refuses to do so. We must know whether the child has *demonstrated* the ability or whether those reporting that they know the child has the ability are merely *surmising* this. In many cases, while a perceived behavioural excess appears to be the problem when a client appears in a clinician's office, a skill deficit is the root cause.

Many children with behavioural excesses, such as overactivity, aggressiveness and destruction of property, have deficits in impulse control and problem solving. It is a disservice to these children to lessen their excesses by the techniques above and leave them with their skill deficits. If we do this, we leave them to face the same problems with no alternatives for resolution.

Behavioural deficits can also be due to skill deficits. For example, a child who is withdrawn and rarely talks in class may lack language skills.

When a skill deficit has been identified as the problem, the next step is to determine whether it is a correctible skill deficit or whether it cannot be corrected with our current level of knowledge. Some examples of correctible deficits are: lack of skills in assertiveness, dating, stress and time management, budgeting, parenting, public speaking, driving and problem solving; also illiteracy in a person whose illiteracy is due to a lack of learning opportunities.

The treatment of these cases consists of training the client in the skill area in which he or she is deficient. This task may be turned over to other professionals or agencies with established expertise in teaching the needed skills, for example, remedial teachers, occupational therapists, special education teachers, adult education facilities, speech and language therapists and budget counsellors.

Uncorrectible skill deficits call for a different approach. Some examples are: attention deficit disorders, aphasias due to brain damage, learning disabilities not due to emotional factors, cerebral palsy and mental retardation. In these cases, since the skill deficit itself cannot be fully remedied by teaching, the goal of therapy is to compensate for the deficit in some way. This might be through the teaching of alternative skills; teaching in a different manner (teaching lip reading and sign language to the deaf, for instance); ameliorating the problem pharmacologically and teaching specific skills (for example, giving methylphenidate for an attention deficit disorder combined with 'stop and think' training); or by means of environmental management. Examples of the latter are directing a person with a severe deficit in the ability to learn arithmetic towards a career that has nothing to do with numbers; adapting a home or institution to be wheelchair accessible; placing children with language deficits in trade and vocational school settings; providing for children who have difficulty ignoring distracting stimuli small classes with minimal extraneous stimuli.

Behavioural deficits

At the other end of the spectrum we find clients with behavioural deficits. A behavioural deficit exists when a person is able to perform a useful behaviour but does so at too low a rate, intensity or duration. Again, we must distinguish between a failure to perform due to lack of skill, in which case the diagnosis should be that of a skill deficit, and the ability to perform a skill but failure to do so.

We must ask questions such as: Is the child withdrawn because of the lack of basic social skills, or does the child demonstrate these skills at home but not at school (or vice versa)? Has the child demonstrated the skill in the past but fails to do so now? If the skill is demonstrable, we must then determine whether the behavioural deficit is due to a lack of reinforcement of the behaviour, a reinforcement of the absence of the behaviour, the presence of a punishing contingency, or conflicting goals.

Sometimes, a behaviour that is desirable does not occur simply because it has undergone an extinction procedure, perhaps inadvertently. A child growing up in the ghetto may be raised by loving and caring parents who teach a number of skills that in most circumstances may be adaptive. However, when the child tries to use nonaggressive conflict-resolution strategies with peers, these may fail because the peers lack similar skills and hence the use of the skills goes unrewarded. A child may do well in school, only to see brothers and sisters who did well in school be unable to go to college due to lack of money and unable to find work because of lack of opportunity or prejudice. This may lead such a child to stop using his or her academic skills and make statements such as: What's the use, it won't get me anywhere anyway!' ('Why should I perform behaviour X when it won't be reinforced anyway?')

We hear similar complaints during marital therapy and parent-child counselling. ('Why don't I tell her what's bothering me?' 'Why should I?' 'She never listens anyway!') Parents may present with a child who doesn't talk. Perhaps both parents have been very busy lately and every time the child has approached them to talk they have politely but firmly said: 'Not just now, I'm busy.' The result might be that the child eventually stopped trying because the efforts were not rewarded. Further, in this case, the absence of the behaviour may be inadvertently reinforced. The parents may have noticed the child was not talking and started attending to the child when there had been prolonged periods of silence. They may have attempted to cajole the child to talk, then when the child did talk to them they were relieved and reverted to their ignoring behaviour until there was another long period of silence. Over time, the child learns (though perhaps being unable to verbalise it) that silence is rewarded and talking is ignored.

Similarly, a teacher may give marks for completed work but only give her personal attention and offer help when children are not working. Or children may be punished every time they try to talk to someone and then generalise this to other settings. A girl, for example, may never speak up in class because every time she has done so at home her mother has yelled at her not to interrupt her television programmes. Children may refuse to fight or break rules, thus demonstrating the skill of self-control. Yet when they do so they may be ridiculed by other children and called 'sissies' or 'goody-goody two shoes', and other children may refuse to play with them.

When failure to reinforce the performance of a behaviour is the problem, we must intervene in the patient's environment to ensure that the appropriate response is reinforced. When reinforcement of the absence of the behaviour is the problem, we must arrange for the reinforcement to be ended and the active performance of the behaviour rewarded. When an adaptive behaviour is being punished, we will usually try to eliminate the punishing consequences.

Conflicts

Sometimes, more than one type of consequence is in effect and the person must choose between the competing consequences. This creates a conflict that can cause a behavioural deficit. The concept of conflict is not foreign to behavioural approaches but differs from 'conflict', as the term is used in psychodynamic theory. Behaviourists use the term 'conflict' to describe situations in which subjects must choose between two or more competing goals. Such conflicts can generate behavioural deficits either through causing the person to be frozen into inaction by having two goals of equal value to choose from, or by choosing a goal that may not be obvious to others and results in a behavioural deficit that is disturbing to others and possibly to the subject as well.

These conflicts can themselves be classified according to whether the person wishes to approach a goal or avoid a perceived undesirable outcome. We all deal with many of these conflicts in our everyday lives. What may be different for the client is the relative value attached to the goals in question.

The following *types of conflict* may be encountered:

Approach-approach
This exists when there are two or more goals the person wishes to achieve, but to approach one involves moving away from the other(s). We meet such conflicts in many plays and books, for example, that of the romantic triangle in which a person must choose between two equally attractive potential partners. Such conflicts may lead to social withdrawal. Unable to choose between partners, the individual may withdraw or vacillate endlessly between the possible partners.

Sometimes children at school feel they must choose between good marks and social acceptance. The result may be a drop in their marks as they choose acceptance over achievement; or their performance may be spotty as they vacillate between the two equally valued goals.

Avoidance-avoidance
Here the subject can only avoid a negative event by approaching another negative event. We have many eloquent metaphors for such conflicts: 'He was caught between the devil and the deep blue sea'; or 'She was caught between a rock and hard place'; or 'He had to choose the lesser of two evils.'

Here are some examples of this type of conflict:

- An employee is asked to engage in unethical behaviour or be fired.
- A child is forced to choose between fighting and being called a chicken.
- A rape victim must choose between going out of the home and facing the fear of repeat rape or staying cooped up in the house.

Approach-avoidance
In this conflict, the problem is that a desired goal cannot be approached without also approaching an outcome the person wishes to avoid. Most dieters know this dilemma intimately. They feel they cannot eat rich food (approach) without weight gain (avoidance). Or they feel they cannot lose weight (approach) without depriving themselves of the foods they prefer (avoid-

ance). A person who is in love with someone of whom his or her family disapproves faces this dilemma. Such a person cannot marry (approach) without losing the approval of his or her family (avoidance). Some children whose parents only seem to give love and affection after they have punished the child create a conflict for the child who must endure punishment (avoidance) in order to obtain affection (approach).

Gradients

Learning theory sees goals as having 'gradients'. The stronger the attractiveness of a goal, or the greater the repulsion from a potential consequence, the greater the gradient. An analogy is a marble resting on a tiltable surface. The more the surface is tilted, the faster the marble will roll, the direction of the tilt determining whether the marble will move towards or away from some point on the surface. Thus the more attractive a goal is, the greater the gradient towards that goal becomes – just as the momentum of the marble increases with greater tilt. And the less desirable an outcome is felt by the subject to be, the greater the gradient away from the consequence and the stronger the motivation to avoid the consequence.

Conflict is created when the gradients are close to being equal. The steeper the gradients, the greater the conflict. The conflict between marrying a person you love or making a career move that will triple your income but takes you to a city where the person you love cannot follow, is a greater conflict than having only 25p in your pocket and having to choose between two chocolate bars.

The concept of gradients is important in clinical practice because one way to resolve conflicts of this nature is to change the gradient of one or more of the goals. We frequently do this with children, as when we help them examine the value of the goals they are pursuing. For example, we may say to a child: 'Do you really want to be friends with children who will only like you if you act stupid?' or 'Does he *really* care about you if he'll only be your boyfriend if you sleep with him?' or 'I know we told you not to fight, but you do have the right to defend yourself if the other kids hit you first.'

In working with children in a weight-control clinic one of us (Douglas Murdoch) sometimes alters the gradient towards attractive foods by explaining what really goes into some foods, such as hotdogs! In many cases, we don't necessarily alter the actual goal or consequence at all. What we do alter is the patient's perception of the goal, the meaning or value it has for the patient. One might ask: 'Do you really want four ounces of fat globbed on to rough crystals of sugar and mixed with chemicals you might stick in a test tube at school (a chocolate bar)?'

Failure of discrimination learning

There is another type of behaviour problem which we sometimes come across. Some behaviours are problematic because of where or when they occur rather than because there is too much or too little of them. A mundane example is that of a child who yells once in a while when in the playground and also yells once in a while when in the house. The behaviour (yelling) is acceptable in one setting (the playground) but not in the other (the house). The child has failed to make a discrimination between the settings, treating them as equal when they are not. A less trivial example is afforded by the case of the professional boxer who is paid to display aggression within the confines of the ring, but who fails to contain aggression in other areas and gets arrested for assault in a public place.

The problems with discrimination fall into two groups. First, a behaviour can occur in too wide a range of situations; in other words, it can be overgeneralised. Secondly, it can occur in too narrow a range of situations; in other words, there is a failure to generalise as much as is needed. The area of social skills provides excellent examples.

First, let us consider the problem of overgeneralisation. One man may be very witty in a crude way and enjoy great social success in the gymnasium changing room and with his casual male colleagues. Yet if he carries that behaviour over into dating situations, he may experience a distinct lack of success. Likewise, a rude style of humour with business clients may cost him sales. If he does not recognise that different behaviour is reinforced in different social contexts, he may well be mystified that his social success is not more widespread.

Children with peer problems often make the mistake of over-generalisation. A boy may be a hero in his sports team because of his aggressive approach to the game and may try to win similar praise by fighting in the neighbourhood and in the school grounds. He may thus win the reputation of bully and the social sanctions that go with that label.

At the other end of the spectrum we see children who are socially inept and imitate behaviour for which they have seen other children reinforced, but they either perform this in inappropriate situations or they have picked the wrong role models. A weak girl may try to imitate the bullying style of a larger, stronger girl and win ridicule and a few bruises for her efforts. A boy may imitate a socially successful girl and earn the label 'sissy' instead of the label he was seeking – that of a 'popular' individual. A child may hear a joke laughed at but repeat it at the wrong place or time (such as when the joke is about the sexual habits of travelling salesmen and the audience he chooses to tell it to is the local parson!).

At the other extreme, we have the case of the person who is capable of performing a behaviour but fails to do so in all the situations in which it is called for. This is a specific, distinct form of behavioural deficit. The failure to generalise can be rather narrow – the behaviour being absent in only a few situations – or widespread – the behaviour not being performed in a number of situations in which it should occur.

One example of a failure to generalise is the child who is obedient at home, but not at school. Such a child may even verbalise the failure to discriminate by saying to the teacher: 'I don't have to do what you say because you are not my mother or father – so there.' Another example of the failure to generalize is that of a person who can be assertive and forthright at work but not at home with his or her spouse and children (or vice versa). The examples we could give are legion.

If the problem is one of overgeneralisation, then stimulus control training is in order. Stimulus control training consists of measures designed to cause the behaviour to occur only when certain conditions are present. This is achieved by ensuring that the behaviour is only reinforced in contexts in which it is desired and not in any other situation. A girl who at school frequently gets out of her seat will probably be very disruptive to the class. If her behaviour goes unchecked, she may well be heavily reinforced by social contact with other children, access to books and games, school supplies and other things. In this case the behaviour 'getting out of seat' is not under any discriminant control. In these circumstances, 'verbal permission from the teacher' will probably be the stimulus we will want to control the behaviour. The result would be that when 'verbal permission from the teacher' is given, the behaviour occurs, and when 'verbal permission from the teacher' is not given, the behaviour 'getting out of seat' does not occur.

In this case, the procedure would be to ensure that the only time 'getting out of seat' is reinforced is after 'verbal permission from teacher' has been given. This may require no more than the vigilance of the teacher who requires our wandering lass to sit down immediately after getting out of her seat (thus preventing any reinforcement); and to wait for permission to get out of her seat, then ensuring that a reinforcement occurs when she does wait. This reinforcement might be praise, social time, access to a special set of materials, or something else that would be effective for this particular child. In other cases, especially where the teacher's attention may be one of the reinforcers that maintains the child's 'getting out of seat' behaviour, it may be necessary to make the contrast between the reinforcing consequences of waiting for permission even greater. This might be achieved by mildly punishing the failures to wait for permission, for example, by the use of 'time out from positive reinforcement'. This might be as simple as a very short stay sitting on a chair away from the rest of the children and their activities.

If the problem is a failure to generalise the behaviour to new and appropriate settings or cues, then the procedure we use is stimulus generalisation training. In this procedure, the person is systematically reinforced at a very high frequency of reinforcement (for example, FR 1 or close to it) in each of the settings in which we wish the behaviour to occur, even though in the setting(s) in which it is already established it may be maintained with much more infrequent reinforcement. As the behaviour is established in each new setting, the rate of reinforcement is gradually diminished to maintenance levels.

In scientific investigations, the above procedure is often carried out sequentially, so that the process occurring can be clearly demonstrated. For example, the behaviour will be reinforced in new setting 1, but not in settings 2, 3 or 4. Once it is established in setting 1, only then is it reinforced in setting 2, while it is still monitored in settings 3 and 4 (which will probably show little or no change in the rate at which the behaviour occurs). Once the behaviour is established in settings 1 and 2, it is then reinforced in setting 3, and so on. In day-to-day clinical work, we tend not to have the time and resources which are often available in research situations. We therefore usually undertake the generalisation training in all desired settings at once.

Chapter 8

Steps in Behaviour Therapy

Clients entering therapists' offices have one characteristic in common: some aspect of their behaviour, overt or covert, has caused discomfort, either to them or to others. Someone, the client or the referral agent, seeks to have that discomfort reduced and perceives a need for some type of behaviour change in order to relieve it. The perceived need for change may be in someone other than the subject. The behaviour change sought may be to take some medication not currently being used, to think differently, to have other people treat the client differently, to act with confidence instead of fear, to achieve a reduction in blood pressure, and so on endlessly.

Regardless of theoretical orientation, the therapist will seek to understand the behaviour so that it will become predictable and controllable: predictable, in order that the therapist may know under what circumstances to expect the aberrant reaction; and controllable so that the aberrant reaction will be eliminated, replaced by an appropriate reaction, reduced, or in some way compensated for by another behaviour.

These are the goals, even of the nondirective therapies, since those treatment methods aim to give clients control over their own difficulties, a therapeutic stance that is compatible with behaviour therapy and, indeed, should be the preferred goal.

All therapists will perform some sort of assessment designed to lead to a treatment plan. The treatment will then have either a beneficial effect, a detrimental effect or no effect. Where therapists differ is in where they look in seeking to understand the behaviour; this, in turn, leads to their use of different methods in their attempts to bring about the desired changes in behaviour.

Psychoanalytically orientated therapists will look at behaviour, not as the focus of the assessment but as providing information about the unconscious functioning of the client's mind. The behaviours of clients and the statements they make are important only in so far as they are signs or symptoms of underlying difficulties. Such therapists will also attend to behaviours that behaviourally orientated therapists rarely consider, for example, dreams – which are considered by psychoanalytically orientated therapists to be windows to the unconscious.

Biologically orientated therapists also view behaviour as a sign or symptom. They tend to regard the problem behaviour as a sign or symptom of an underlying organic or biochemical disorder; this may suggest that a particular medication, surgical procedure or other physical treatment will bring about helpful changes in the neurological functioning of the client, and thus lead to a resolution or amelioration of the symptoms.

Nondirective therapists also view behaviour as a sign or symptom of underlying and probably unconscious processes. They differ from the psychoanalysts only in perceiving their role as helping their clients interpret their own signs and symptoms rather than themselves providing the interpretations.

The behaviour therapist views the client's behaviour as a *sample* of the difficulty much as a physical scientist might take a sample of soil into a laboratory for analysis. The behaviour itself is what is important, not what it might symbolise.

Contrary to popular belief, this does not mean that behaviour therapists necessarily deny the existence of the unconscious; it is rather that they deny that it is accessible to an external observer in a manner which allows reliable and accurate measurement. This means that it is not a proper focus for analysis if we are to take a scientific approach to our work.

Since behaviour therapy seeks to be the applied arm of a science of human behaviour (as we explained in Chapter 1), the unconscious remains outside this approach for now. The behaviour therapist seeks to understand any behaviour by focussing on the particular situations in which it occurs, the responses available to the client and the thoughts, feelings and perceptions the client can report.

The possibility exists that psychoanalytical formulations might be incorporated into behavioural approaches at some time in the future. If this is to happen, however, these formulations must be operationally defined, reliable measurement must be possible, and the validity of the measurements must be established. This is because behavioural approaches require that scientifically proven principles be applied to the assessment and modification of human behaviour. Hence, any approach which conforms to these standards is acceptable. No hypothesis about human functioning need be ruled out of order, provided that it is based on scientifically acceptable data.

The behaviour therapist's approach to therapy reflects the methodology of an experiment in many ways. In an experiment, there are two kind of variables: the dependent variable and the independent variable. The independent variable is the one which the experimenter changes in a precise and carefully planned way. An experimenter will administer precise amounts of a drug to investigate the effects of dose levels. The dose of the drug used is the independent variable. Alternatively, two different drugs might be administered and their effects compared. The two drugs are the independent variables. Other examples of independent variables might be two different ways of teaching mathematics or the presence or absence of a child care worker.

The dependent variable is the one which is not manipulated or varied by the experimenter. It is observed and changes that occur as a result of the manipulation of the independent variable are noted. The hypothesis on which the experiment is based concerns the relationship between the independent variable and the dependent variable. By varying the independent variable and measuring the effect, if any, on the dependent variable, we determine the nature of the relationship. We can then use this information to predict events and gain a measure of control over them.

X The purpose of assessment within this model is to collect data that will allow us to generate an hypothesis about how the problem behaviour is being maintained. We begin by taking a broad overview of the situation. We are interested, of course, in what brings the client to our office on that particular day. We are also interested in the client's prenatal, perinatal and postnatal history, developmental milestones, academic performance, medical history, significant social experiences such as family dissolution or the deaths of important others, parenting history, perception of childhood (or childhood to date) and so forth. We are interested in these matters not because they may reveal unconcious conflicts or arrested stages of development but because of what they may tell us of the following:

- The behavioural strengths and weaknesses the client brings to the situation.
- Possible physiological and intellectual limitations on learning.
- Past and current opportunities for learning.
- The probabilities that particular types of behaviour will occur.

The history may also suggest to us that the presenting problem of the client and the one we feel needs to be addressed are not one and the same. In other words, we start with a broad, general look at the ways in which the client functions and decide how best to respond. We may decide to continue seeing the client or to refer the client elsewhere, and if we are to offer treatment we decide on the direction therapy should take.

Taking this broad view of the client and the client's difficulties enables us to start developing the behavioural hypothesis; it helps delimit the parameters within which we will be working. At the risk of oversimplifying, the parameters of our approach with a five-year-old child will be quite different from those that apply when we deal with a 35-year-old account executive.

The next step is to enter into a narrower, more focussed phase of the assessment. The goal here is to arrive at a specific behavioural formulation of the client's difficulties, including the behaviours which are to be the targets for change. The therapist proceeds to identify the target behaviour and perform a detailed analysis of the circumstances that evoke and/or maintain it, with a view to developing a behavioural treatment.

The therapist has a wide range of measures of the target behaviour to choose from, depending on the nature of the behaviour and whether it is a single behaviour (a single dependent measure) or multiple related behaviours. In the latter case we must deal with multiple dependent measures, as we might have to do when treating a patient presenting with depression.

The therapist's choice will also depend on whether the target behaviour is directly observable (for example, smoking, hitting other children or social contacts); or is accessible only through the report of the client (as, for example, with obsessional thoughts, sad affect or irrational beliefs), or by physiological measurements (as of blood pressure, stomach acidity or resting muscle tension).

The choice of a target behaviour is equivalent to choosing a dependent variable. The identification of the antecedent stimuli and the consequences that maintain the behaviour are equivalent to identifying the independent variables. The hypothesised relationship between the dependent and the independent variables is the experimental hypothesis, and treatment is the systematic manipulation of the antecedent and consequent conditions. The outcome of the treatment is the test of the hypothesis. If the treatment is successful and there is the predicted change in the target behaviour, the hypothesis is confirmed. Therapy is then either terminated or it moves on to another problem area.

Assessment procedures

A key aspect of the above procedures is the continuous monitoring of the target behaviour throughout the process. This helps us establish that the changes in the target behaviour are related to changes in the treatment. There is a wide choice of data collection methods open to therapists at each stage of the process. These can be grouped into *indirect*, *analogue* and *direct* methods of assessment.

Indirect methods of obtaining data include all methods which do not involve observing the behaviour directly in the environment in which it normally occurs. They include behavioural interviews, questionnaires and self-report inventories. Some of these techniques target a single behaviour. Some target multiple behaviours hypothesised or demonstrated to be related to a common construct, such as anxiety or depression. Yet others cover a wide range of behaviours and are especially useful at the screening (problem identification) stage, and for monitoring for beneficial or undesirable side effects of treatment. (An example of a beneficial side effect is a decrease in symptoms of anxiety and depression after social withdrawal is reduced. An undesirable side effect would be an increase in aggressive behaviour following a reduction in social withdrawal.)

Reports by parents or teachers of children's behaviour, when these are not based on the systematic and careful measurement of the behaviour, are other examples of indirect methods of assessment. Even self-report, either during an interview or in response to a questionnaire, should be considered indirect if it is not based on a period of careful and systematic self-monitoring. In general, people are poor reporters of their own behaviour except perhaps when they are specifically attending to it as a means of assessing it.

Analogue assessment refers to the assessment of behaviour in a contrived setting or manner that has some resemblance to the situation in which the difficulties naturally occur. Role playing is a good example of analogue assessment. The client and the therapist assume roles and the therapist assesses how the client behaves. Two (or more) clients in a group may also engage in role playing.

Another example of analogue assessment is giving a parent and a child a task to complete while trained observers monitor their interaction. The same technique can be used with married couples. Almost any assessment done in an inpatient clinical setting will be an analogue assessment by default.

Direct assessment occurs when the behaviour is assessed directly in the situation in which it naturally occurs. This can be done by the therapist, by trained observers, by significant people in the person's life such as parents, teachers, spouses or co-workers, or by the subject himself or herself. Another option is to measure the behaviour mechanically or even telemetrically.

Direct assessment is an ideal that is strived for but never achieved. Any 'direct' assessment is in reality an analogue assessment, since by introducing the observation we have altered the situation in some way, whether the observation is done by the subject, by someone already in the environment, by someone introduced to the environment or by a mechanical device.

The Heisenberg uncertainty principle in physics states that one cannot assess without altering the situation. You can know the speed of a particle or its direction but not both, since to assess one you necessarily alter the other. It is much the same with the behavioural assessment of a person, for the moment you assess, you have altered the situation and cannot know for certain how things would have proceeded had you not assessed. This concept is called reactivity. The behaviour reacts to being assessed. Smoking is a good example of this principle. Most smokers, when they first start to self-monitor the number of cigarettes they smoke and/or the interval between cigarettes, show a marked decrease in the number of cigarettes they smoke.

Baseline measures

Once you have determined your dependent measure and the means of collecting data on it, the next step is to establish a baseline. A baseline is a stable pretreatment level of the behaviour to which the changes produced by treatment are compared to see if there has been any change. Without a baseline it is hard to know whether there has been a change.

Take the three graphs shown in Figs 8.1, 8.2 and 8.3 of an excessive behaviour problem. If these are graphs of the treatment phase, then it would appear that Fig. 8.1 shows successful treatment, Fig. 8.2 shows no change and Fig. 8.3 shows that the

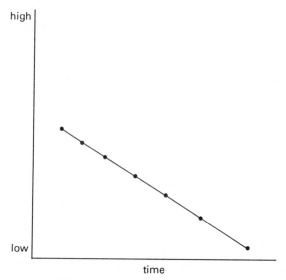

Figure 8.1 Excessive behaviour problem decreases.

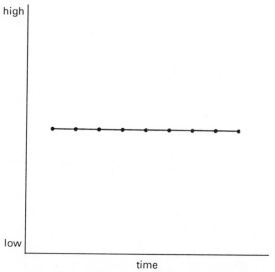

Figure 8.2 Behaviour problem unchanged.

treatment actually made things worse. However, now let us look at the three graphs again, but with a baseline period added to each (Figs 8.4, 8.5 and 8.6).

It is clear now that Fig. 8.4 shows that the treatment had no apparent effect whatsoever. The behaviour was already decreasing

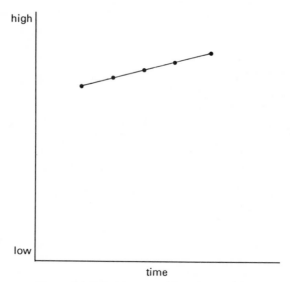

Figure 8.3 Behaviour problem increasing.

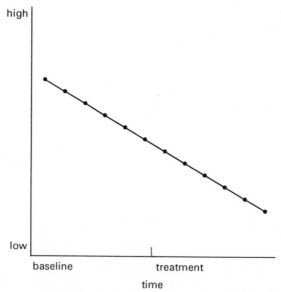

Figure 8.4 Steady decrease: treatment irrelevant.

during the baseline period and the treatment did not accelerate this decline at all.

It is also now clear from Fig. 8.5 that the straight line indicated a successful or at least partially successful treatment rather than no

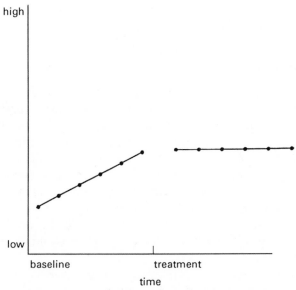

Figure 8.5 Treatment halts increase in behaviour problem.

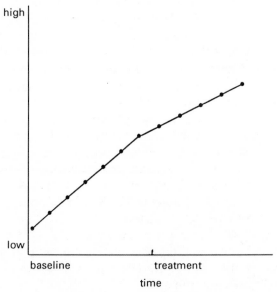

Figure 8.6 Treatment slows increase behaviour problem.

effect, since it clearly had the effect of arresting the acceleration of the behaviour and stabilising it at a set level.

Finally, it now becomes clear that, rather than having a dele-terious effect on the problem behaviour, the treatment in Fig.

8.6 had the effect of slowing the rate of increase of the undesirable behaviour.

The treatment phase

Once the target behaviour has been selected, a means of measuring it has been devised and a baseline established, it is time to implement the treatment that is implicit in the hypothesis that has been generated. If, for example, our hypothesis is that a young adult's social avoidance is due to a skill deficit, namely a lack of assertiveness, the client might be asked to record all social contacts outside of work during a four-week period. Let us assume that there are no contacts during the first week, two during the second, and one during each of the last two weeks. The baseline is thus relatively stable, varying between 0 and 2 over a four week-period.

Treatment is initiated which involves assertiveness training, concentrating at first on the skills of meeting people, and initiating and maintaining conversation. The client is asked to continue to monitor the number of social contacts during this phase. The week following the first treatment session, he makes two contacts, the second week three contacts and the fourth week five. By the twentieth week following the first treatment session, he is averaging ten contacts a week and treatment is terminated, this rate of making contacts having been jointly predetermined by the therapist and the client as acceptable.

According to some texts on behaviour therapy the above constitutes insufficient evidence that the intervention was responsible for the change that occurred. Although there is a single point of change in the rate of the behaviour at the time of the initiation of treatment, it is possible that some other factor was responsible. Possibilities are that the subject acquired a telephone or spontaneously starting using a deodorant, for example.

Authors who take this latter point of view will often advocate that you should return to the previous conditions and then repeat the treatment. If the behaviour returns to baseline levels when baseline conditions are reinstituted and then again shows improvement when the treatment conditions are reinstituted, this clearly demonstrates that the treatment was effective and that the hypothesised relationship between the target behaviour and the antecedent and consequent conditions did indeed exist. While there is scientific merit to this position, in practice it presents serious practical and ethical problems. Certain behaviours would be injurious to the client or to others if allowed to return to baseline levels, for example, head banging, smoking and fireset-ting. Various ways of overcoming this problem are described by Hersen and Barlow (1976) in *Single Case Experimental Designs*.

Summary

In summary, a behaviour therapist approaches a patient's behavioural difficulties much as an experimental scientist approaches an experimental problem. Each develops a notion about the relationship between two variables and devises a way to see whether that relationship does indeed exist. They then carefully measure the variables in question under the conditions necessary to test their hypothesis. If the hypothesis is confirmed, the problem is solved and knowledge is added to our general fund of knowledge (or the knowledge of our patient). If the hypothesis is not confirmed, then it is changed and the process repeated until the problem being studied can be predicted and controlled. This comparison between a scientific experiment and the steps taken in behaviour therapy is illustrated in Table 8.1.

Table 8.1 *Comparison between an experiment and behaviour therapy*

Experiment	Therapy
Choice of area to be studied	Client presents for therapy
Literature search and basic delineation of parameters	Screening and general disposition
Identification of dependent variable(s)	Choice of target behaviour(s)
Hypothesis generation	Hypothesis generation
Choice of independent variable based on hypothesis	Choice of treatment based on hypothesis
Experimental phase	Treatment phase
Continuous monitoring	Continuous monitoring
Evaluation of results	Evaluation of results
Repeat if hypothesis not confirmed	Repeat if hypothesis not confirmed
Next experiment if hypothesis is confirmed	Terminate and next client or next target behaviour with same client if hypothesis is confirmed

Chapter 9

Behaviour Therapy for Anxiety Disorders and Depression

In previous chapters we have looked at the components of behaviour therapy. We must now consider how these components are put together in clinical practice.

Twenty years ago, it would have been behaviouristic heresy to approach this task by looking at diagnostic clusters in a text on behavioural approaches. Today, most cognitive-behaviour therapists accept the commonly used psychiatric diagnostic terms. This means that we can now be reasonably sure that in doing comparative psychotherapy studies we are all treating similar problems.

Yet another factor may have helped promote the greater use of diagnostic categories. In its early days, behaviour therapy addressed individual behaviours in isolation; it viewed each new instance as a unique case, since every person would have a unique learning history. This applied even though similar techniques might be used over and over again. But it came to be recognised that certain types of behaviours tend to occur together. This has been established empirically with children (Achenbach and Edelbrock, 1983), adolescents (Achenbach and Edelbrock, 1979) and adults (Millon, 1987).

It has also been found that there are certain commonly occurring types of behavioural excesses, deficits and skill deficits, and also cognitive errors. It therefore became possible to use the concept of diagnosis without discarding basic behavioural thinking.

This chapter will illustrate how the components previously described are put together in comprehensive behaviour therapy programmes, using the examples of anxiety disorders and depression. The following two chapters will use, as further illustrations, addictive disorders and disruptive disorders of childhood. In each case we will first look at the disorder from a behavioural point of view. We will then look at the cognitive and behavioural approaches to treatment. In many cases we will gloss over or even ignore other factors and treatments, such as the biological. This is not because other treatments do not have their place but because we wish to maintain the focus on the cognitive-behavioural approach, rather than on the disorders we are considering.

Anxiety and stress-related disorders

Anxiety is a widespread problem in our society and the many self-help books on how to cope with stress and the anxieties of every-day living are testimony to this. Anxiety is also a feature of many mental health problems. Some of the therapeutic approaches we will consider may therefore be useful adjuncts in therapy. The focus in this section is on those disorders in which anxiety is the central feature. There are many anxiety disorders that share at least some characteristics in common, for example, agoraphobia, social phobia, panic disorder, simple phobia, obsessive compulsive disorder and separation anxiety.

What is anxiety? It is hard to define. Everybody seems to know what it is, but there is no universally accepted definition. A reflection of this difficulty is that even by 1961 there were over 120 specific procedures available which, it was claimed, measured anxiety (Cattell and Scheier, 1961). This is at least in part because anxiety is actually a complex reaction which may involve any or all three of the modalities of behaviour (motor, cognitive/affective and physiological).

The following are the components of anxiety we need to deal with, using the three modality model of motor behaviour, cognition and affect, and physiological (autonomic) responding.

(1) The motor component

The motor component of anxiety reactions reflects the basic be-havioural choices facing all life forms capable of locomotion – fight, flight or freeze. The responses of freeze and flight are the two most commonly associated with anxiety in our society and in diagnostic thinking but, in some cases at least, aggression seems to be a response generated out of fear of a perceived threat.

The 'flight' response is more commonly referred to in cognitive-behavioural writings as the escape and/or avoidance response. The subject attempts to leave the anxiety-provoking situation and will avoid that situation if at all possible (flight in anticipation). This can provide a useful measure of the anxiety. The subject is asked to approach the feared situation and a direct measurement is taken of how close the person can approach it. When people are actually able to engage feared objects or situations, we might time how long they can stay in contact with feared objects or stay in feared situations.

An example of the above is the case of a young boy seen by one of us (Douglas Murdoch). He could not be examined by a physician because of his fear of medical procedures and instruments. As a measure of his fear, he was taken to a play room and asked to get as close as he could to different elements of a toy doctor's kit. We then used a string to measure how close he was.

Similarly, the strength of the motor component of an agoraphobic's fear might be measured by timing how long the subject can remain out of the home, or by the distance the person can travel from the front door. As an example, a severe agoraphobic was so fearful of leaving her home that the initial measure was of how long she could stand just inside the front door looking out.

The avoidance response can be quite dangerous. One of us (Douglas Murdoch) was assessing the strength of a phobia of driving near water by having the patient drive along a boulevard next to a river. The driver began to shake and displayed motor avoidance, causing the car to veer into the oncoming lane. After several oncoming cars swerved on to the shoulder with horns blaring, the test was considered complete! Further assessment was conducted in the therapist's office in comfortable chairs with the client *imagining* the feared situations.

Alternatively, or in addition to escape responses, a person may freeze when confronted with a situation perceived as threatening. This can be a literal freeze as in the person who is 'scared speechless'. As an example we might take the child who knows the answers at school but cannot speak when called upon in class. Or the freeze may be more figurative, as with a person who fails to execute a necessary emergency procedure when faced with an anxiety-provoking situation or object. An example of this is the person who drives straight into an oncoming car rather than swerving to avoid it, or the man who fails to administer first aid to an accident victim, despite having the necessary knowledge, because all he can do is stand and stare shocked at the sight of the blood.

The flight and freeze responses may be mixed. Or the response may be more subtle as is the case when the motor component is manifested by a disruption of motor processes. This occurs when people cannot perform complex motor behaviours in anxiety-provoking situations, despite their ability to perform well in non-anxiety-provoking situations. An everyday example is the weekend golfer who might usually sink nine out of ten four-foot puts but miss nine out of ten when playing in an important competition. One of the key skills professional athletes must acquire is the ability to control their motor responses and retain the integrity of complex motor sequences (such as those involved in hitting a tennis ball) in anxiety-provoking situations (such as the fifth set at Wimbledon).

The motor component does not always have to be as dramatic as panicky flight, studious avoidance or lashing out in aggression. The motor response to an anxiety-provoking situation may be nothing more than restlessness or fidgeting, as evidenced by inability to sit still, excessive and unnecessary movements (such as pacing), or playing with objects (such as tapping a pencil, or twirling or fingering a bracelet).

(2) The cognitive/affective component
We gain access to this domain through self-report. We know people are anxious because they tell us so, one way or another. They may report unease, vague discomfort, worry, anxiety or abject fear. One of the best ways of assessing patients' percep-tions of their fear is to use a 'subjective units of distress' scale. This simply asks subjects to indicate their degree of distress in a variety of situations on a scale of 0 (totally relaxed) to 100 (extreme discomfort). Alternatively, the scale is anchored by 0 (totally relaxed) and 50 (as scared as you've ever been) and with no upper limit. Some therapists add a metaphorical element and use a 'fear thermometer'; they may actually give the client a paper and pencil drawing of a thermometer on which to indicate their degree of discomfort.

There are many more or less sophisticated self-report scales which are used to measure 'anxiety'. Most of these tap not only the affective and cognitive components of the anxiety, but also self-report measures of the motor and physiological changes. One of the most widely used is the State Trait Anxiety Inventory which has both an adult version (Speilberger *et al.*, 1970) and a children's version (Speilberger, 1973).

Cognitive theory assumes that cognition and affect go hand in hand, with the cognition preceding and determining the affect. The common element in all anxiety reactions is the perception of some type of threat. One can be anxious about a real and tangible threat most bystanders would also identify, or the perception and attributions about the degree of risk may be unrealistic to most bystanders.

We usually refer to this latter situation as a 'phobic reaction'. Beck (1976, pages 161–2), states:

'The label phobia is warranted only when the person greatly exaggerates the probability of harm and experiences distress disproportionate to the real risk.'

Beck has thus identified one of the cognitive errors that can be associated with anxiety as overestimation of the actual risk. Many other dysfunctional cognitive processes also seem to be associated with the arousal of anxiety. Even when real risk exists, these types of thoughts can prevent optimal coping.

An important contributor to the anxiety reactions is the cognitive error of 'catastrophising' (Ellis, 1962). This is the tendency to embellish a situation with more danger than actually exists and to dwell on the imagined potential consequences. Consider two drivers on a motorway. Both are somewhat preoccupied and wander slightly out of their lanes. In each case, a car in the next lane gives a warning honk. The first driver says to himself: 'I must be more careful and concentrate on driving.' The second driver says: 'Oh my God, I was almost killed and I almost killed that other driver too. I'm an absolute menace on the road today and I'm stuck on a motorway. What am I going to do?' Guess which one is going to have the anxiety attack in a few moments and possibly become a true menace!

Another common error is repetitive thoughts about danger (Beck, 1976). The subject has frequent verbal thoughts or mental images of the anxiety-provoking situation. These serve as false alarms.

Beck (1976, page 151) identifies stimulus generalisation as a further component of what he calls 'thinking disorder in anxiety'. This is really the cognitive error of arbitrary inference, in which a conclusion is drawn despite insufficient evidence to support it. In an example given by Beck (1976), a woman hears a siren and assumes her house is on fire while visualising her family trapped inside. Beck also states that such subjects are not afraid of the situations or objects concerned, but of the anticipated consequences of being in contact with those objects, or in those situations. Hence it is the meaning given to the situation that brings on the anxiety, not the situation itself. This involves the attribution or misattribution of threat.

The cognitive elements which characterise anxiety disorders are the forms of the thought processes. The different anxiety disorders differ, however, in the content of the thoughts. Indeed, this differs from phobia to phobia (Beck, 1976). For example, in agoraphobia Beck (1976) has found that the common content is a fear of losing control and being humiliated and/or a fear of encountering difficulties away from home and being unable to obtain help from anyone. In acrophobia, the content of the fearful thoughts is fear of falling and sustaining severe injury. A common element in the fear of lifts, tunnels and aeroplanes is anticipation of a malfunction of some kind removing the protection, so that that the structure will collapse, crash or deprive the person of necessities of life such as air, food or water.

(3) The physiological component

Anxiety can manifest itself in physiological functioning in various ways. The pattern seems to be idiosyncratic, different physiological subsystems being more or less likely to respond in anxiety-provoking situations in different individuals (Selye, 1974). We all recognise this in ourselves and in our clients. Some people have 'nervous stomachs', others get palpitations, still others are susceptible to tension headaches.

Accurate measurement in any of these modalities is difficult because of the technical problems and potential confounding factors that can mask the results (Bernstein, 1981).

(4) Domain specificity

A complicating factor in assessing and treating anxiety reactions is the relative independence these three response systems can exhibit (Bernstein, 1981). This harks back to Chapter 3 and the emphasis on the need to assess all three response domains.

Cognitive-behavioural interventions

Cognitive-behavioural interventions may be grouped into five types:

(1) Promoting approach responses

The motor component of the anxiety reaction can be viewed as a behavioural deficit in approach behaviours. The logical interventions therefore are those which will result in an increase in approach behaviours. Approach behaviours are increased through modelling (the therapist or someone else demonstrating approach responses) and shaping (rewarding successively closer approaches to the feared object).

Alternatively, the anxiety can be understood using the classical conditioning model of behaviour. The fear is seen as a conditioned response to a conditioned stimulus (the feared object or situation). Repeated exposure to the feared object, either in a controlled hierarchy (systematic desensitisation) or all at once (flooding), is an extinction procedure and leads to the reduction or elimination of the conditioned response (anxiety) in the presence of the conditioned stimulus (the feared object or situation). The avoidance of the feared object prevents the patient from undergoing the extinction process more normally.

(2) Skill enhancement

In some subjects, the anxiety can be understood as the by-product of a skill deficit. The interventions then used are those which will enhance the client's skills.

The most common skill taught in order to reduce anxiety is the ability to relax on demand. Relaxation can be taught in several ways. Which one is used will depend on the skills and preferences of the therapist and client factors. Some of the more widely used methods of teaching relaxation are progressive relaxation, autogenic training, biofeedback, imagery and meditation.

Relaxation is not the only skill taught to combat anxiety. Not far behind in frequency is the teaching of assertiveness skills. This is actually a group of skills combining complex motor behaviours, including speech, and cognitions. The aim of these programmes is to teach clients to stand up for their rights, while respecting the rights of others (Alberti and Emmons, 1974; Lange and Jakubowski, 1976).

Some clients need a wider range of interactional skills to alleviate anxiety. For them, social skills training will be used. The aim of social skills training is to identify systematically the deficits in social interaction skills and remedy those lacks. The deficits can be in such basic skills as making appropriate eye contact and having nonverbal behaviour congruent with verbal, to the more subtle and complex skills of social problem solving, reciprocity and negotiation.

Other skills which might be taught to alleviate anxiety include time management, role playing, problem solving and 'stop and think' training.

(3) Cognitive reappraisal and restructuring

The manifestations of anxiety in the second dimension of behaviour – cognitive/affective – can be corrected using the techniques of cognitive therapy that were discussed in Chapter 6. The cognitions may change as a result of behaviour change as well. The experience of success in approaching the feared object or situation may well result in a reappraisal of the beliefs the patient had developed.

Some of the more common cognitive techniques for dealing with anxiety disorders are challenging irrational beliefs by evaluating the evidence for the belief, modifying imagery, reducing anxiety about anxiety and restructuring assumptions (Beck and Emery, 1985), systematic desensitisation in imagination, implosion (Bernstein, 1981), and thought stopping (Steketee and Foa, 1985; Kaplan, 1986).

(4) Establishing voluntary control over 'involuntary' processes

The actions of the autonomic nervous system were once considered automatic and unmodifiable. Therefore little attention was paid to nonpharmacological ways of modifying the actions of this system. It was hoped that altering motor behaviours and cognitions would result indirectly in changes in the 'involuntary' system. But the pioneering work of Miller (1969) and others has shown that autonomic functions can be controlled by the same operant principles as motor behaviour. From this discovery has grown the whole field of biofeedback – the detection, amplification and representation to the subject of such autonomic processes as heart rate, blood pressure and muscle resting activity levels. Contingent consequences are then administered, either by the therapist or by the patient. These techniques can be used to deal with some of the more somatic manifestations of anxiety.

(5) Primary and secondary prevention

Another way of dealing with anxiety is to prevent it building up in the first place or, once it is detected, to intervene quickly to minimise the potentially adverse effects it can have. This is the purpose of the many stress-management programmes that are available. One of the leaders in the prevention of anxiety and minimising the impact of anxiety-producing situations has been Meichenbaum (1985), with his 'stress inoculation training'. Two other examples of stress-control programmes are those of Rosenthal and Rosenthal (1985) and Selye (1974).

Depression

Much attention has been paid to depression in the behaviour therapy and cognitive-behavioural literatures. Here we will first look at depression to see how it can be understood using a behavioural diagnostic formulation. We will then consider how we may intervene in the light of this formulation.

Components

(1) Motor

Various motor behaviours are associated with depression. First, there is a generalised motor behaviour deficit. Depressed people simply do less. This is usually a performance deficit, the depressed person not performing behaviours that were previously performed. There may be failure to perform the acts necessary to maintain personal hygiene, a decrease in eating behaviours, a decrease in work-related behaviours or, in severe cases, a widespread, generalised performance deficit so that the person lies in bed all day or sits in a chair for hours on end. There is usually a decline in social behaviours. The person initiates fewer contacts and fails to provide or respond to conversational cues.

Another feature of the motor behaviour may be a decrease in the speed with which motor actions are performed, whether these be gross motor acts such as walking, or fine motor activities such as writing or speech production. On the other hand, patients with 'agitated depression' show an excessive amount of motor action. Nonverbal motor communication behaviours such as body posture and facial expression may show behaviour excesses such as slouching, frowning, crying and gaze aversion. There may be behavioural deficits in smiling, assertive postures and eye contact.

There may also be deficits in more complex behaviours such as assertiveness, social skills, job skills and parenting skills. Goal-directed behaviours may also be in a deficit state. Food intake may be increased, rather than decreased. Suicidal behaviour may be a particular concern.

(2) Cognitive/affective

Few would deny the importance of cognitive processes in depression. Central to depression is excessive negative evaluation by patients of themselves, their hopes for the future and their ongoing experiences. These in turn (especially the negative expectations for the future) may lead to thoughts of suicide. Depressed persons perceive themselves to have experienced an excessive amount of loss, real or imagined. Such distortions can reach delusional proportions. There are cognitive deficits such as inadequate sampling of the information available, so that patients fail to perceive positive events that occur.

Depressed persons also display skill deficits in their thinking, such as a failure to generate and test hypotheses adequately. There may be such errors in thinking as overgeneralisation, arbitrary inference, selective abstraction, dichotomous thinking, magnification or minimisation, and personalisation. There may also be deficits in more complex cognitive processes such as social or general problem solving.

(3) Physiological
Some of the physiological problems that occur in depression are impaired sleep function (any of hypersomnia, insomnia, frequent awakenings, early morning awakenings), weight gain or loss, decreased sexual desire and impaired appetite.

Cognitive-behavioural interventions

The focus in the past ten years has been on the cognitive aspects of depression and its treatment. However, even 'cognitive' approaches address the depressed person's behaviour (Beck *et al.*, 1979).

(1) Increase the frequency, duration and intensity of motor behaviour that is incompatible with depression
The goals here are:

- To increase activity levels.
- To provide the experience of pleasure and mastery.
- To provide the patient with the necessary skills, especially to prevent relapse.

One way of achieving these goals is to get patients to keep activity diaries and then to ask them to increase their levels of activity. They are also asked to record activities as pleasurable experiences, mastery experiences, or neither. They are then instructed and rewarded for increasing the frequency, intensity or duration of the pleasurable and mastery experiences. This fits in both with the cognitive model of depression and with the theory that a contributing factor can be a low rate of response-contingent positive reinforcement (Lewinsohn, 1974) – though the role of contingent reinforcement as a cause of depression remains un-proven (McLean, 1981).

(2) Alter the cognitions hypothesised to be maintaining the depression
This is currently considered to be the core of the cognitive-behavioural approach to treating depression.

There are several aspects of this process to be considered. Its es-sence is a joint examination by therapist and patient of the latter's beliefs, assumptions, perceptions, attributions and imagery, to test their validity and change them as necessary. Cognitive-behavioural therapists teach depressed patients to be 'scientists', in that they learn the techniques of hypothesis testing and logical analysis. At the start, patients may need to be taught to recognise and monitor their automatic thoughts, before any re-evaluation of these thoughts can occur. Knowledge of what are the subject's automatic thoughts helps establish which underlying beliefs and assumptions need to be examined. It also helps to bring to light the cognitive errors that need to be addressed. The therapist may need to do some teaching here as well.

(3) Where necessary deal with underlying physiological problems directly
Medication cannot be considered a behavioural intervention and many behaviourally orientated therapists would be quick to point out that one of the purposes of developing cognitive-behavioural approaches to treatment is to eliminate the need for chemical management. Nevertheless, there seems in some cases to be a strong biological predisposition towards depression (Allen, 1976). In addition, the medical investigation of patients with depression is necessary to ensure that they do not have such conditions as hypothyroidism or mononucleosis.

(4) Provide a social and physical environment that decreases the likelihood of a depressive response
Emphasis on patients' internal cognitive states may lead us to overlook their environments. Yet the latter may profoundly affect their behaviour.

Environmental factors that may be involved range from the immediate social environment to the season of the year. Therapy might include family sessions as a focus or an adjunct to therapy. Work with the family might address such issues as the amount and type of feedback the patient receives from the family, the role the patient plays within the family, shared dysfunctional cognitions and communication styles (Bedrosian, 1988).

In the course of therapy the patient may decide, as a result of examination of the issues, that a change of employment, residence, social group or marital status is necessary. It may become clear, as therapy evolves, that the patient's physical or social environment – or both – are impoverished. Greater physical stimulation or a wider social support network – or both – may be needed. A period of treatment in hospital may be necessary to provide sufficient control over the environmental conditions.

(5) Prevent the successful completion of suicidal behaviours
All of the above are worthless if the patient does not survive long enough to benefit from the therapist's expertise. Therefore a critical aspect of any treatment of depression must be adequate measures to prevent the completion of suicidal wishes. At the extreme this means admitting the patient to hospital involuntarily.

A person who has recently moved into a new place of residence and has not established social connections to the community may be quite isolated. Or the patient's social network might be such that an adequate degree of supervision and support is unavailable. This may be because of problems afflicting other family members, because the family system is dysfunctional, or both. The environment itself may be dangerous, as in the case of battered women and children. In such cases removal from the home may be necessary (and perhaps sufficient) to bring about a reduction in the suicidal wishes of the patient.

The therapist or the clinic may fill in for environmental deficits by being an extended and temporary support system for the patient. This function can sometimes be performed by 24-hour crisis services. Some communities try to enhance the social environment by providing crisis phone numbers and crisis centres to meet this need.

Suicide prevention only begins with environmental manipulation, however. The real work involves addressing the depressive cognitions and behavioural deficits that maintain the suicidal thinking.

Further reading

There is an extensive literature on the subjects we have dealt with in this chapter. We recommend the following references: Beck *et al.* (1979); Beck and Emery (1985); Meichenbaum (1985); Kazdin (1989); Barrios and O'Dell (1989); and Matson (1989).

Chapter 10

The Behavioural Treatment of Addictive Disorders

Behaviour therapists have contributed extensively both to research in the area of addictive disorders and to the treatment of these disorders. Their role has been controversial at times and they have tended to abandon the disease model of addiction.

The behaviourist sees addiction as a learned behaviour pattern. Therefore treatment must teach more appropriate behaviour patterns. In the case of alcoholism, the issue of whether controlled drinking is possible is a controversial one (Sobell and Sobell, 1976; Marlatt, 1983). We need not try to resolve it, however, to present most of the treatment issues. The controversy concerns only the goals of therapy and the criteria for success. These are areas in which further research is needed (McCrady, 1985).

Components

(1) Motor components

Addictive disorders, by definition, involve behaviours which fall into the category of behavioural excess. Indeed, it is the excessive quality that distinguishes the addictive user of a psychoactive chemical from the recreational or medical user of the same drug. The definition of 'excessive' creates problems, however. How much is too much? In practice, the definition is an idiosyncratic one. Consumption of the chemical is considered excessive when the consumption results in impairment in the subject's ability to function. The therapist is concerned with the combination of impairment of functioning and a demonstrable dependence, either physical or psychological, on the substance. (The legal definition of excess is another matter.) In practice, it is hard to distinguish where problem drug use ends and addiction begins. It is probably better to view them as existing on the same continuum, requiring similar approaches to treatment.

The excessive consumption of a psychoactive substance is

rarely the only behaviour problem with which an addict presents. Indeed, it is often because of other behaviour problems – correctly or incorrectly attributed to the substance abuse – that the person is referred or comes for treatment. Parenting skills may be deficient. Assertiveness skills or more general social skills may also be impaired. There may be deficits in impulse control or in the expression of certain emotions such as anger and sadness, failure to eat adequately, job skill or money management deficits, and so on. The substance user may have either true skill deficits, never having acquired certain skills prior to the addiction, or performance deficits, having at one time demonstrated the skills but no longer doing so. Whether the performance deficit is due to the process of addiction or not would be a matter for assessment.

There may also be behaviour excesses that need to be addressed. These, too, may be causally related to the addiction, or independent. Some of the excessive behaviours associated with addictions are undue social withdrawal, excessive verbal and physical aggression, criminal behaviour, excessive risk taking behaviour and suicidal gestures.

(2) Cognitive/affective components

Cognitive processes have been less well studied in the addictions than they have in anxiety and depressive disorders. It has been demonstrated that prolonged exposure to some of the substances of abuse (such as alcohol) can lead to organic brain damage and permanent impairment of certain cognitive functions, notably memory. The role of cognitive deficits and distortions in the aetiology of the addictions is less clear. Addicted individuals sometimes present with anxiety or affective disorders for which the substance abuse was an attempt at self-medication. In these cases, one would expect to find similar motor behaviour and cognitive and physiological deficits and distortions as in other cases of anxiety and depression. If these are found, they are treated accordingly.

Even when there is no diagnosable anxiety or affective disorder, there may still be cognitive and affective difficulties. It is quite likely there will be a problem-solving deficit. The subject may hold inaccurate beliefs about the effects of the substance(s) being used, or about himself or herself. Indeed, some of the effects attributed to alcohol are in reality due to people's beliefs and expectancies and the environmental cues (Abrams and Wilson, 1979; Graham, 1980; Graham *et al.* 1980; Pihl, 1983; Murdoch, 1985).

(3) Physiological components
A major feature of the physiological response is the nervous system's accommodation to the abused substance. This results in craving and withdrawal symptoms.

Cognitive-behavioural interventions

The interventions used with addictive disorders follow the SORC model quite closely (McCrady, 1985). Some cut across modalities and deal with such complex behaviours as assertiveness in various situations, while others are quite specific (such as addressing quantity and frequency of 'sips' in a problem drinker).

(1) Change the association of alcohol
The objectives here may be twofold. One may be to condition an aversion to alcohol, using classical conditioning techniques. The second may be to change the patient's expectations about the consequences of drinking.

The first and somewhat controversial approach to changing the associations of alcohol is to use aversion therapy and pair the presentation of alcohol with an aversive event. The aim is to make future presentations of alcohol elicit a negative conditioned reaction which will lead to the avoidance of alcohol (hence it mixes classical and operant procedures). The presentation of the alcohol is usually paired with administration of either an emetic or an electric shock. The procedure is controversial because it inflicts pain and suffering in the client in order to bring about the 'cure'. It is not commonly used, however, because it is not entirely effective and the procedures to make it effective can be laborious. The main problem is a lack of generalisation. If you classically condition a vomiting response to the presentation of gin, for example, it often does not generalise to other forms of distilled liquor, let alone wine or beer. It becomes necessary therefore to condition the nausea and vomiting to every possible source of alcohol in a sequential manner.

The other component of a behavioural approach to changing the associations is an educational one. The pharmacological effect of most abused substances is quite rapid. We know that consequences which occur very quickly after a behaviour have more impact in altering behaviour than do consequences that occur some time after the behaviour. The reinforcing qualities of the pharmacological properties of the substance therefore have far more impact than do the later adverse consequences, such as ill health, marital conflict and financial problems. One component of treatment can be to make these later consequences more salient to the client. At the Alexandra Clinic in Oshawa, Ontario, for example, patients complete worksheets to calculate the financial cost of their alcohol problems in the past year, both the direct cost of the alcohol and the indirect costs in lost wages, increased insurance rates, fines, lawyers' fees, broken and lost material goods and so on. The clients also take stock of the social costs of their addiction.

(2) Educate to compensate for knowledge deficits about the drug
Sometimes patients have surprisingly little knowledge about the drug they are abusing. It is necessary to educate them about its effects and its hazards. This may be especially important when patients are misattributing actions to the drug, thus reducing the need for them to do anything about the problem so attributed.

(3) Remove the deficits for which alcohol compensates
Patients usually display some behavioural deficits for which they use alcohol to compensate: 'I can't talk to women unless I'm stoned' or 'I can't relax without a beer'. It is necessary to help such patients acquire the skills they lack and, most importantly, get them to recognise and accept that the performance of the skills does not depend on their having alcohol in their system.

   Among the specific therapy techniques that may be needed are assertiveness training, relaxation training, communication/social skills, dating skills, career counselling/retraining, stress-management training, or training in job interview skills, time management, organisational skills or problem solving.

(4) Remove the environmental factors which buffer the person from the consequences of the addiction
Some patients do not really experience the full consequences of their addiction, because one or several people are buffering them from those consequences. It might be a wife who tells the boss her husband is sick when he is really on a bender or in bed with a hangover. It might be the husband who gets up early and makes breakfast and lunches for the children and then stays up late at night to do the housecleaning and laundry that didn't get done because his wife was in a drugged stupor. It may be a sympathetic boss who overlooks the absenteeism out of friendship, even when it is hurting the company. In these cases, it is necessary to

bring a halt to the rescuing. This may be done through family counselling or individual therapy with the rescuer.

In other cases it may be necessary to work closely with employers to develop integrated programmes which encourage treatment but do not rescue the employee.

(5) Create new patterns of behaviour and environments not associated with substance abuse

The associations between certain environments and behaviours and the excessive use of the abused substance may be so strong that it is practically impossible for the patient to remain in those environments or participate in those activities, even after treatment. Patients are often faced with the need to give up these activities and even to disassociate themselves completely from social contacts strongly connected with their addictive behaviours. It may be difficult for them to accept that they must do this, but if they do not they risk relapse.

Alternative environments, social contacts and activities need to be found. An important aspect of treatment is therefore leisure counselling, career counselling or intensive social skills work to establish new support networks not based on substance abuse – or a combination of these.

(6) Establish a safety net/alternative to the substance abuse for times of stress

Many studies have linked stress and substance abuse. Stressful situations are also more likely to result in relapse after treatment is completed. It is therefore necessary to provide patients with stress-management skills, and some safety nets to call upon should they feel the need. This may involve turning to someone in the family, or to a friend, or the use of a crisis phone line or drop-in service. It may involve having evening drop-in 'booster sessions' so that clients can come back as the need arises. For many, joining a fellowship such as Alcoholics Anonymous or Narcotics Anonymous is helpful. All these are intended to provide physical and social environments that will promote non-addictive methods of coping.

(7) Restructure the cognitions and beliefs that support the substance abuse

This theme repeats itself across diagnostic categories, so we will not deal with it in any depth here. It is worth mentioning, however, that a characteristic cognition that needs to be addressed with substance abusers is that the entire cause of their addiction, and therefore the entire cure, lies outside the patient: 'If only my wife (husband) would stop nagging me (show me more affection), I wouldn't have to drink' or, 'If my parents weren't so hard to get on with, I wouldn't have to use these drugs'.

It must be established with the patient that Problem A (which may or may not exist) does not directly and irrevocably cause Problem B. The patient can choose methods of coping other than substance abuse to deal with Problem A (nagging spouse, rigid parents).

(8) Preplan to deal with relapse

In this budget plan tour of behavioural approaches to dealing with addictive disorders, the last stop is an important one. One characteristic of the behavioural pattern associated with addictions is relapse. It is necessary therefore to plan for what the patient will do in the event of a relapse. This is really a matter of secondary prevention.

If the relapse cannot be prevented in the first place, how can the patient minimise the damage caused by the relapse and get back into the nonaddictive behaviour pattern as quickly as possible? This aspect of treatment has been well covered in *Relapse Prevention* (Marlatt and Gordon, 1985). It has many components but central to them is the development of a plan of action involving carefully thought out and rehearsed behaviours and cognitive strategies which are invoked by the cue of the relapse.

Further reading

We have here only outlined behavioural approaches to addictive disorders. Useful sources of further information include McCrady (1985); Marlatt and Gordon (1985); and Schlesinger (1988).

Chapter 11

Disruptive Disorders

Children are more often referred to mental health clinics because of disruptive disorders than for any other reason. The revised third edition of the American Psychiatric Association's *Diagnostic and Statistical Manual* (DSM-III-R) (American Psychiatric Association, 1987) subdivides these disorders into conduct disorders, oppositional defiant disorders, and attention-deficit hyperactivity disorders. The problems subsumed under these diagnostic headings are generally resistant to change and no therapy currently available can claim a high rate of success. Behavioural approaches have shown some promise, however.

Components

Following the format we have been using, we will look at the disruptive disorders first by considering the three major response channels. In the interests of brevity we are considering these three diagnostic groups together. The operational definitions in DSM-III-R (American Psychiatric Association, 1987) indicate which of the behaviours belong to which diagnosis. In practice, however, there is much overlap between the categories, and dual diagnoses are not infrequent.

(1) Motor components
When children with these disorders are first seen, most of the identified problem behaviours are motor behaviours that fall into the category of behavioural excesses. The behaviours can be excessive in any one or all of the dimensions of frequency, intensity and duration. Take, for example, aggressive behaviour. A boy may be referred because he hits other children frequently but usually only once and without injury. Another child might have assaulted only two children but be referred because she has left

both with serious injury. Another child might be referred because his aggressive outbursts (temper tantrums) last for hours when they do occur. Of course, it is common for children to be referred because their behaviour presents problems in more ways than one.

Many motor behaviours may occur in excess in children with disruptive behaviour disorders. These are well illustrated in the behaviours that make up the three externalising factors of the Child Behaviour Checklist (Achenbach and Edelbrock, 1983). Among these, the commoner ones are impulsivity, aggression (verbal and physical), theft, firesetting, destruction of property, remaining in close proximity/contact with others with similar difficulties, running away, missing curfew and forcing others into sexual conduct.

(2) Cognitive/affective components

The cognitive aspects of the disruptive disorders have been less well studied than the motor and family components. They have also been studied less than the cognitive aspects of the more internalising disorders, anxiety and depression. Kendall and Braswell (1985) have suggested that the problem underlying the impulsivity which is so characteristic of this group is a cognitive deficit, not a distortion as is assumed to be the case in depression and anxiety. While risking oversimplification, we may say that the deficit is in the ability to use self-instructional language to modulate and regulate behaviour – to stop and think before one acts.

The predominant affective state tends to be sadness. This is not invariably so and some children show no pervasive abnormality of mood. Some even seem to take pleasure in inflicting pain.

While hard data are lacking, we have the clinical impression that children with disruptive disorders have some cognitive distortions. One of these is the perception or belief that they have special status at one extreme or the other. Either they believe they are entitled to special treatment or they believe they are exceptionally bad (or unlucky) and can only expect negative things to happen to them.

Another cognitive distortion of these children seems to be the expectation, either that they will not get caught when they violate a norm of society, or that they will not experience an adverse consequence. Hence they feel they can act with impunity. They also tend to become angry when these expectations are not met and blame those imposing the consequences for their discomfort, rather than recognising them as the results of their own actions. They tend to see the application of punishment as arbitrary and malicious, rather than contingent and instructive.

Alternatively, these children have the expectation that only negative consequences will occur following their actions. Good behaviour has not been rewarded (and hence has undergone an extinction procedure or was never shaped in the first place), and bad behaviour may result in a positive outcome (power over peers, acquisition of material goods if stealing is successful). While their misdeeds may have undesirable outcomes, if these children are caught, in essence they feel they have little or nothing to lose.

Sometimes these children seem to believe that in violating the norms of the wider society they are bringing about personal or group justice. ('What have you ever done for me/us?' or 'Society owes us' or 'People who aren't like us are the reason things aren't better for us. If we don't get them they'll get away scot free.')

Another central aspect of these children's cognitions is often a lack of endorsement of more widely accepted social norms. These children either do not recognise or refuse to accept the principle of reciprocity. They believe in 'finders keepers/losers weepers'. They do not recognise or accept the need to inhibit oneself when interacting with people who are weaker in some way – it's okay to hit people smaller/weaker than yourself. Many seem to have adopted a philosophy of 'survival of the fittest/buyer beware' (except when they are the buyers) – even if they cannot articulate such beliefs. Certainly there is a deficit in their ability to trust others.

Other distortions and deficits often encountered include the belief that it is a catastrophe if things are not as the young person thinks they should be; unwillingness to delay gratification; difficulties in the perception of social stimuli; and deficient social problem solving.

(3) Physiological components

There is some evidence that physiological factors play a part in the aetiology of these disorders. This is probably strongest in the case of attention deficit disorders. Antisocial behaviour tends to run in families and polygenic inheritance may play a part (Vandenberg et al., 1986, Chapter 10). There is also a higher then expected incidence of learning disabilities in this group of children. But whether or not children with disruptive disorders react differently physiologically has not been well investigated.

Cognitive-behavioural interventions

(1) Improve external controls

In a sense, the behaviours subsumed under the heading disruptive disorders are 'out of control'. In fact, this is not the case if we work on the assumptions of behaviour therapists, who believe that all behaviour is controlled by the interaction of the environment and the person. Thus the question is not whether the behaviour is under control, but rather: 'What influences are controlling the behaviour at the time in question?'

When we say a child's behaviour is out of control, we are really saying that the child is not performing the desired behaviours, nor have those responsible for the child been able to create the appropriate contingencies to promote more desirable behaviour. One goal therefore is to establish an environment in which the contingencies exist which are needed to bring about a reduction of the inappropriate behaviours, and an increase in the desired behaviours. This necessitates working with the child's physical and social environment rather than with the child directly.

In extreme cases, it may be necessary to alter radically the child's physical environment through admission to an institution. This may apply when a child's behaviour creates serious risk to himself or herself, or to others, and control cannot be established quickly in the community. The advantage of an inpatient or other institutional admission is that it provides a high degree of control over the physical and social environment of the child, so that relationships between variables can be observed. It is useful to have staff who are trained in the techniques of systematic behavioural observation to accomplish this. It is especially helpful to have at least one staff member whose sole responsibility is to perform this function.

Another advantage of an inpatient admission is that it can restrict the child's access to problematic environments (for example, shops from which the child may steal, and environments low on supervision). The child can be reintroduced to these environments gradually and systematically, as control over the problem behaviour is established.

Less intrusive, and therefore preferable, is alteration of the child's physical and social environment on an outpatient basis. This may involve moving the child from a normal classroom to one specifically designed (physically, socially and educationally) to deal with problem behaviour. Such a classroom will probably have a greatly reduced student to teacher ratio; a reduced total number of students; staff who are specifically trained in behavioural approaches to child management; the necessary facilities to administer adequate and humane consequences (rewards and costs) for behaviour; and a curriculum that is individually tailored to the needs of each child. There should be available a range of desirable activities as rewards, and sufficient space to allow short periods of social isolation or a 'time out' room.

At home, changes in the physical environment might range from minor alterations in the availability of certain problem items (such as locking up the drinks cabinet) through moving the child to a new room to separate problem siblings, to a complete change of neighbourhoods due to the unhelpful influences of the child's current community.

The changes in the social environment of the child will probably be brought about by one or a combination of the following:

- Parent training.
- Marital therapy.
- Family therapy.
- Teacher training/consultation.

The aims of such therapies include:

- Increasing the quantity and improving the quality of the monitoring of the child's behaviour.
- The reinforcement of desired behaviour.
- The modelling of good communication, problem solving and prosocial behaviour.
- The acquisition by the child of skills.
- Decreasing the reliance on coercive techniques by the authority figures involved.
- Decreasing, or ideally eliminating from the child's environment, the modelling of the inappropriate expression of anger and sadness, poor communication and deficient problem-solving skills.

In summary, the aim is to produce an environment which promotes and models prosocial behaviour and discourages anti-social behaviour, by the use of non-coercive techniques.

(2) Improve self-control
Addressing the hypothesised deficit in self-control is often a major part of the therapy. This is often easier to accomplish once

there is adequate external control over the child's behaviour. There are several ways of assisting children to establish control over their behaviour.

The first step is to get children to attend to their own behaviour. In clinical settings it is often remarkable to hear children with disruptive disorders complain that another child did something to them, and then describe how they themselves did almost exactly the same thing, without recognising that the two behaviours are quite similar. At first, self-monitoring may be improved by environmental manipulation such as having a staff member label the behaviour and then tell the child that he or she is engaging in that behaviour whenever it occurs.

An example of the above is afforded by the case of a child seen in our inpatient unit. He was constantly interrupting but did not seem to be aware of this. His mother had identified this pestering as similar to being hounded by a woodpecker. The child's primary nurse therefore labelled this interrupting with persistent requests and questions, 'Woody behaviour' (after the cartoon character 'Woody Woodpecker'). Whenever the boy began to pester someone the nurse, in a matter-of-fact way, would tell him he was using his 'Woody' behaviour again – also that Woody behaviour was ignored here, an extinction procedure.

The next step was to get the child to identify the behaviour himself. So after a while the nurse would ask the child what he was doing rather than tell him. The child would respond: 'Oh yeah, I'm being Woody again'. The nurse might have to add, 'And what do we do about Woody behaviour?' – to which the child would reply either 'You ignore it' or 'I'm not supposed to do it'. Next we would try to get the child to identify the behaviour himself without being cued ('Oops, I'm being a Woody again'), and finally covertly to catch the mental preparation preceding the problem behaviour and to inhibit the expression of the behaviour so that it does not occur.

Self-monitoring alone is often not enough, just as having parents simply note good or bad behaviour is unlikely to alter a child's behaviour. Feedback is important to behaviour but it is consequences that determine behaviour. The essence of self-control, then, is for children to recognise the consequences of their behaviour and act accordingly. One also tries to get them to deliver the reinforcers and punishments to themselves. ('I got 29 out of 40 on my maths test – that's a real improvement for me. That extra studying paid off. I'm really proud of myself.' 'I got 10 out of 30 on my spelling test. I should have studied last night instead of watching the television. I won't watch any tonight and I'll study for an extra hour to make up for it. I don't want to get 33 per cent again.')

Self-monitoring and self-reinforcement are insufficient if the child lacks the necessary skills or behaviours. The therapy to develop self-control may therefore include such skill and behaviour-building interventions as anger management training, assertiveness training and social skills training.

Kendall and Braswell (1985) have included many of these techniques and more in their comprehensive treatment programme for impulsive children. The core of this programme is the addressing of the impulsive nature of the behaviours by getting the children to stop and think about what they are doing, what is required of them in that situation, what the options are and what the consequences might be, and then to proceed in a planned manner, evaluating the outcome for future reference.

(3) Eliminate/compensate for deficits

Many children with disruptive disorders, more than in the population at large, also have learning disabilities. It is therefore necessary to address deficits like these with interventions such as remedial education, special school placement or even residential care. Sometimes the deficits are in the parents and it may be necessary to provide in-home helpers/aides/trainers, or to place the child temporarily outside the home while the parents are acquiring the necessary skills. In the most unfortunate of cases, where the parent(s) cannot or will not acquire the necessary skills, permanent removal of the child from the home may be necessary.

The place of formal diagnoses

We have illustrated in this chapter and the two preceding ones, and in an introductory way, the cognitive-behavioural approach to the assessment and treatment of some of the more common problems presenting to clinicians in clinical settings. The process of behavioural diagnosis is not necessarily incompatible with making a diagnosis according to DSM-III-R (American Psychiatric Association, 1987) or the International Classification of Diseases (World Health Organization, 1978) but demands a higher degree of specificity. It is also more concerned with the context of the behaviour. The latter point means that patients with similar behaviours (that is, similar formal diagnoses) may end up receiving very different treatments. However, it is likely that the treatments will be related in some way, and will be drawn from similar classes of treatments.

Further reading

This chapter has provided only a brief outline of the behavioural approaches to the treatment of disruptive behaviour disorders. The following references deal with the subject in greater depth: Patterson (1982); Kendall and Braswell (1985); DiGuiseppe (1988); Barkley (1989); and McMahon and Wells (1989).

Chapter 12

Behaviour Therapy and Interactional Problems

In previous chapters we have discussed the cognitive-behavioural approach to the treatment of disorders falling into some common diagnostic categories. These methods have wider applications, however. We will outline some of their further uses in this and the following chapters.

The use of behavioural approaches is not limited to individual subjects. If behaviour is determined by its consequences, then it is possible to look at the interactional nature of human behaviour to see how the actions of one person influence another and vice versa. There is a fast-growing trend in the behavioural field to view behaviour in its ecological context and from a systems perspective (Mash, 1987). The functional nature of behaviour is maintained in this perspective which, however, also considers the behaviour of the system of which individuals are part. The 'system' can be any group of two people (husband-wife, parent-child, supervisor-supervisee, teacher-pupil, peer-peer, sibling-sibling, and so on), or more (nuclear families, multigenerational family units, school classes, work places, sports teams, treatment teams, and the like).

Behaviour therapy and the family unit

Behavioural marital therapy

A 'system' commonly seen by clinicians is the marital dyad. In working with marital couples the therapist must consider the behavioural excesses and deficits of the dyad as a unit as well as the behavioural excesses and deficits of the husband and wife as individuals.

Let us take the example of problem-solving skills. Individually, the husband and wife might have good decision-making skills. His might be demonstrated in his leadership role in the local union. She might display excellent problem solving in her work as a bank supervisor. Yet the couple may have difficulty solving problems together, due to a lack of mutually compatible problem-solving skills or some other block. Behavioural approaches that address such systems problems have been in use a number of years, pioneered in large part by Neil Jacobson (1977).

When marital couples present for treatment, they often complain of rather vague symptoms of distress, rather than coming with specific behaviours which can readily become targets for therapy. 'Distress' is a short form for 'an amalgamation of observable and unobservable behaviours' within the behavioural framework (Jacobson and Dallas, 1981, page 380). This is used in assessment by relating the degree of satisfaction and dissatisfaction each member of the marriage is experiencing to the specific behaviours that are occurring. This means that behavioural approaches to marital therapy with distressed couples should use a cognitive-behavioural model, since this relates cognitive and affective states (distress) to behavioural events.

Despite the above, basic behavioural concepts are still important. Thus it has been shown that the degree of satisfaction a member of a couple feels on any given day is strongly related to the number of rewards and punishments received from the partner on the same day. Furthermore, at least one study has shown that the absence of reinforcement and the relative predominance of punishment precedes the marital distress. Moreover, members of distressed couples tend to pay more attention to punishment from their partners and to be relatively unaffected by reinforcement, whereas members of satisfied couples tend to be attentive to and affected by the prevalence of positive reinforcement from their spouses and unaffected by their negative behaviours (Jacobson and Dallas, 1981).

A difficulty met with in applying the behavioural model to marital problems is that of identifying which behavioural events should be the target behaviours – that is, which are the antecedents and which are the consequences. The use of these terms assumes a perspective, namely that there is an identified patient, with an identified problem, and that other people in the social environment provide the antecedents and the consequences. In all likelihood, each partner is more than ready to identify the other partner as the person with the problem and insist that the partner's behaviour change. In reality, it is the marital unit that has the problem, each partner making unique contributions to this. We are thus dealing with reciprocal influences. The partners' behaviours are antecedents, consequences and behaviours simul-taneously. This takes behavioural marital therapy away from the more linear view of causality common to individual approaches to therapy. Causality becomes circular (Jacobson and Dallas, 1981). The principle behind this approach is that of reciprocity (Patter-son and Reid, 1970).

The problems couples face vary considerably and therefore re-quire individual behavioural analysis. Marital satisfaction is the end result of a number of skills. These include the physical expression of caring, communication, child rearing, and house-hold and financial management skills. Deficits in any of these can lead to marital conflict (Jacobson and Dallas, 1981).

Many of the techniques and procedures used in individual cognitive-behaviour therapy are employed in behavioural marital therapy. These include teaching problem solving, self-monitoring, behavioural rehearsal and role play, among others. An advantage behavioural marital therapy has is that the other half of the 'prob-lem' is present, which is rarely the case in individual or even group behaviour therapy. Hence the therapist can get the couple to engage in actual conflict resolution rather than simply in role play. The direct observation of the behaviours in question is possible (allowing, of course, for the bias introduced by having an observer present and, in many cases, by the artificial environment of the therapist's office). Another advantage is that the spouses can monitor each other's behaviour. This can be done systemati-cally, for example, by using the Spouse Observation Checklist (Weiss and Perry, 1979) which is completed daily.

The usual procedure in behavioural marital therapy is to have an extended period (for example, three weeks) of initial assess-ment to allow all the relevant factors to be evaluated. The next step is to engage the couple in the therapeutic process by in-creasing the rate of positive reinforcement between the partners, even if this is done quite artificially at first. Next, the more difficult work of addressing skill deficits is tackled. The final stage is to generalise the use of the skills (if not already accomplished) and gradually disengage by fading out the therapy (Jacobson and Dallas, 1981).

Behavioural family therapy

The potential for the application of behavioural principles to the family unit is not limited to the marital dyad. The entire family unit and the influence of family members on each other can be the focus of treatment. The movement towards this approach has been most notable in behavioural approaches to clinical work with children, particularly in the last ten years. The opening chapter of Mash and Terdal's (1981) text *Behavioral Assessment of Childhood Disorders* was entitled 'Behavioral assessment of childhood disturbance'. The corresponding chapter in the second edition published seven years later (Mash and Terdal, 1988) was 'Behavioral assessment of child *and family* disturbance' (emphasis added).

Mash (1989, page 6) identifies five concepts that characterise current behavioural approaches to child clinical problems:

- The view of child and family disorders as constellations of interrelated response systems and subsystems.
- The need to consider the entire situation when assessing the impact of any single variable.
- The idea that similar behaviours may be the result of different sets of initiating factors.
- A recognition that intervention is likely to lead to multiple outcomes, including readjustments of relationships within the family system.
- The notion that family systems and subsystems possess dynamic properties and are constantly changing over time.

Mash (1989) also notes that the assessment of childhood disorders is becoming increasingly complex, information being obtained from mutiple sources using multiple methods (Mash, 1987; 1988); and that treatment is becoming multicomponent and multidisciplinary (Mash, 1989).

Gerald Patterson and his colleagues (1976; 1982) at the Oregon Social Learning Center have been pioneers in the study of the reciprocal influence of behaviour on family members. They have conducted meticulous and elegant research into the family using an empirical approach based on behavioural principles. They have demonstrated the interactive and contingent nature of family relationships. In particular, they have shown how, in dysfunctional families, the members develop coercive methods of controlling one another's behaviour, through the predominant use of punishment and negative reinforcement, rather than positive reinforcement. They have also shown that these patterns are associated with the development of disruptive disorders. More recently, Patterson's colleagues have documented the distorting influence that psychopathology has on the family interaction patterns, for example, when a family member is depressed.

The family systems aspects of the disruptive disorders are also discussed by McMahon (1987). He lists a number of relevant family variables. These include the parents' skills and performance ('can' versus 'does') in problem solving; monitoring children's behaviours; and the degree to which parents are involved with their children. The personal and marital adjustment of the parents is often critical.

There is a need to separate parents' views of their children from the actual problems with which the children present. Is one dealing with a behaviour problem or a problem with the parents' perception? Depressed parents are more likely to view their children negatively and to act accordingly. In such cirumstances children are more likely to respond with negative behaviour. Open hostility between parents is more common when conduct disorder in a child is the presenting complaint and may be more important in distorting parental perceptions of the child than depression. Finally, the degree of stress the family system faces and the number of supports available outside the home have been shown to be related to the behaviour of mothers towards children with conduct disorder and to treatment outcome.

Patterson's efforts to study and treat families from a behavioural perspective have been joined by a number of other researchers and clinicans in the past decade. Behaviourally orientated family therapists have addressed a wide range of clinical problems. These have included such areas as child abuse (Morton, Twentymen and Azar, 1988); aggression in marriages (Arias and O'Leary, 1988); stepfamilies (Leslie and Epstein, 1988); conduct disorders (DiGuiseppe, 1988); family problems in geriatic populations (Qualls, 1988); addictions (Schlesinger, 1988); depression and suicidal wishes (Bedrosian, 1988); and sexual dysfunctions (Walen and Perlmutter, 1988); marital dysfunction (Bornstein and Bornstein, 1986); and parent-adolescent conflict (Foster and Robin, 1989).

Disorders of sexual functioning

The systematic treatment of sexual disorders is a relatively new area of clinical endeavour. Its start was marked by the landmark publication *Human Sexual Inadequacy* (Masters and Johnson, 1970). This was a largely atheoretical treatise and the field today remains quite eclectic. However, many of Masters and Johnson's techniques can easily be conceptualised and their effectiveness explained using learning theory (Reed and LoPiccolo, 1981). For example, a set of techniques commonly used in sexual therapy regardless of the focal problem are the sensate focus exercises; in these the couple are instructed to take turns giving pleasure to each other in gradually more sexual ways. These exercises bear a striking resemblance to systematic desensitisation exercises and may well serve the same function.

Behavioural and cognitive-behavioural techniques are commonly used by sex therapists. Foremost among them are the array of anxiety-reduction methods developed within the cognitive-behavioural framework. This is because anxiety appears to play a major role in many of the sexual dysfunctions – either aetiologically or as a consequence of the disorder, or both (Delora and Warren, 1977; Kaplan, 1975; Reed and LoPiccolo, 1981).

Some of the instructions given to clients are intended to cause cognitive shifts from a focus on performance to a focus on sensation and giving pleasure. Indeed, it is a common practice to forbid actual intercourse in the first stage of therapy in order to achieve this goal.

Some of the exercises fall directly into the category of skill acquisition – for example, the graded exercises designed to improve control over ejaculation, and the Kegel exercises sometimes recommended to women to improve tone and control over important muscles in the vagina. The therapist will assess the patient and his or her partner for knowledge deficits and address these through education. The therapist should also be a model to the patient (and/or couple) of healthy sexual attitudes, open relaxed communication about sexuality, and if the 'therapist' is in fact a couple, as is sometimes the case, the couple should model healthy heterosexual communication. In addition, they may use modelling of sexual technique within ethical bounds, through the use of models (for example, demonstrating the 'squeeze' technique using a plastic penis), or movies (Reed and LoPiccolo, 1981), or the use of illustrative drawings (Kaplan, 1975).

Cognitive and behavioural techniques become even more important when a problem is not due simply to a skill deficit, as when a man develops premature ejaculation or erectile failure after previously having good functioning, or a woman becomes anorgasmic after a period of being orgasmic. In these cases, the difficulties may be due to a traumatic experience, relationship difficulties, situational problems or dysfunctional attitudes and beliefs that have developed. One also encounters patients with both cognitive impediments to successful sexual functioning and skill deficits. In these cases, promoting cognitive change, teaching problem-solving techniques, marital therapy, operant techniques and desensitisation – all discussed in earlier chapters – are among techniques that may be useful (Reed and LoPiccolo, 1981).

Disorders of sexual development

We make a value judgment whenever we label a behaviour dysfunctional. In many cases, there is general – though rarely universal – agreement that a behaviour or a set of behaviours is dysfunctional or abnormal. Agreement is less general when it comes to sexual development. But many individuals do find their preferences troublesome and anxiety provoking and request treatment to alter these preferences, or to help them to cope with their preference and the reaction of others. There are also preferences which are regarded by most people as not only deviant but intolerable, regardless of the comfort of the patient – for example, paedophilia.

In this section, we will discuss behavioural techniques which aim to alter or help patients cope with sexual preferences that differ from the heterosexual norm.

The earliest interest in behavioural approaches to disorders of sexual development was generated by the apparent superiority of aversion therapy over conventional therapies in eliminating unwanted sexual arousal. Yet the overall clinical success of these techniques was not very impressive. The behaviour therapists dealing with these problems cast a wider net in their assessments and found that arousal to atypical stimuli was only a small part of these patients' problems, and frequently not the one which caused them the most distress. There were often many behavioural deficits in the area of heterosexual interaction (Barlow and Abel, 1981). These patients frequently expressed difficulties in relating to members of the opposite sex, sometimes even when they experienced sexual arousal.

Current approaches to treatment therefore focus on such deficits which are hypothesised to be present in many of these cases. Indeed, Barlow and Abel (1981) report that it is not even necessary to address the issue of atypical sexual arousal in many cases. The treatment involves many of the interpersonal skill-building techniques that have been elaborated upon in several other places in this book.

The most resistant to treatment of the paraphilias is the gender dysphoric syndrome or transsexualism. The major intervention for this disorder has been sex-reassignment surgery (Barlow and Abel, 1981). However, Barlow and Abel (1981) report a successful case of gender reassignment using behaviour therapy in a four-step process.

The client was a 17-year-old male who was ineligible for sexual reassignment surgery even though he wanted it. He agreed to try the therapy with the provision that surgery could still occur later if it didn't work. His history and presentation were consistent with gender dysphoric syndrome. Assessment showed that he experienced arousal to transsexual fantasies but not to heterosexual fantasies, and had 'grossly' inadequate social skills and extreme gender-role deviation.

The first therapeutic step was explicit training through modelling, rehearsal and feedback (praise, correction and videotape replay) of more masculine forms of such motor behaviours as sitting, standing and walking. These behaviours were generalised to the boy's normal environment where they were negatively reinforced (the removal of a stimulus contingent upon the performance of a behaviour – in this case, a reduction in teasing and taunting by peers when the more masculine behaviours were performed).

The next step involved addressing the deficits in heterosexual skills through shaping, chaining and behavioural rehearsal. This was done for interactions both with males and with females since this patient was deficient in both areas. This resulted in improved relations with both sexes but he was still attracted to men and was not aroused by heterosexual fantasies. Next, increasing arousal to heterosexual stimuli was attempted using classical conditioning techniques. (These have subsequently been elaborated on and essentially consist of initially obtaining arousal to a photographic slide of a male then gradually fading out the slide of the male and fading in a slide of a female. Eventually, arousal only to the 'female' slide can be made to occur.)

Finally, at the insistence of the client, aversion therapy was used to bring about a decrease in homosexual arousal. This comprised two components. The first was the pairing of mild electric shocks with homosexual arousal. Then covert sensitisation was used, the patient imagining a homosexually arousing situation and simultaneously imagining an aversive scene.

The treatment used with this boy has since been replicated with two other transsexuals, except that they chose to retain a homosexual orientation and did not undergo the fourth step of decreasing atypical arousal. Barlow and Abel (1981) maintain that the same basic approach can be used with any of the disorders involving atypical sexual arousal. Some of the components of this case presentation have also been used by other authors in successfully dealing with paraphilias (Annon, 1975; Birk, Miller and Cohler, 1970; Cautela and Wisocki, 1969; Edwards, 1972; Herman *et al.* 1974; Stevenson and Wolpe, 1960).

Behaviour therapy and other interpersonal situations

Interpersonal problems are not restricted to close relationships, such as those found in families or between sexual partners. Difficulties relating to other people can themselves be a focus of treatment, or they may need to be addressed as aspects of the therapy of other disorders. For example, difficulties in making or sustaining friendships can lead to a low rate of pleasant events which can contribute to depression. The symptoms of depression such as reduced energy can further reduce the opportunities for interaction, making the person less attractive to others. This further reduction in successful interpersonal contact accelerates the depression, and so on in a downward spiral.

The list of examples does not stop with depression. Dodge (1989) has identified no less than 17 DSM-III-R (American Psychiatric Association, 1987) disorders in which some social incompetence is at least one of the diagnostic criteria. He further identifies nine disorders in which early social incompetence may predict the development of the disorder later in life (such as alcoholism), and 14 more disorders in which social incompetence probably plays a part in the disorder. The pervasiveness and importance of interpersonal problems in psychiatric disorders is underscored by the fact that Dodge was looking only at problems in social relationships in children! Difficulties with social interaction can be problems even when they are not associated with a psychiatric diagnosis. Children who are rejected by their peers but do not have a psychiatric diagnosis often report considerable personal unhappiness and loneliness (Asher and Wheeler, 1985). Just as important, social interaction problems that are not treated are likely to be enduring (Coie and Dodge, 1983).

Problems in nonfamilial interpersonal relationships need to be addressed in the same way as the other problems we have discussed. We need to distinguish deficits in skill from deficits in performance. We need to know whether a problem is pervasive or restricted to particular situations or classes of people (relates well to women but not to men, relates well to co-workers but not to supervisors). We need to know what makes the problem worse and what makes it better. We need to know what happens when a person displays the problem and what happens when the person does not. We need to know of other factors that may contribute, such as physical attractiveness. This is a powerful variable and children or adults who are deemed unattractive may experience rejection even though they possess good social skills. For example, there presently exists in western society a significant prejudice against obese people and this prejudice can be found in children as young as six. It can result in teasing, taunting and ridicule, and in academic, work and housing discrimination (Wadden and Stunkard, 1985).

A therapist trained in behaviour therapy has a wide range of therapeutic interventions available to alleviate social interaction problems in clients, once the nature of the problems has been clearly identified. The two most widely known and used are probably assertiveness training and social skills training.

Assertiveness training is a therapeutic programme with many components. Subjects are taught and adopt assertive beliefs. They identify cognitions that are impediments to acting assertively and replace them with assertive cognitions. Assertive behaviours are taught. The behaviours are both verbal – how to speak assertively – and nonverbal – how to act assertively. The aim of assertiveness training is to allow people to stand up for their own rights while respecting the rights of others. It also aims to allow them to express their feelings freely and appropriately, with respect for the feelings of others but not at the expense of their own feelings (Fensterheim and Baer, 1975; Lange and Jakubowski, 1976).

Social skills training is in many ways more basic than assertiveness training. The skills of social interaction are so well learned for most of us that we take them for granted, and use them automatically and without real awareness that we are using learned skills. Many of our patients have failed to learn these basic skills or, for any one of a number of reasons, fail to use them.

The deficits can be at the most basic of levels. Patients may need to be taught how to make eye contact, how to let a speaker know they are attending and listening, how to show that they are interested in what a person is saying. They may need to learn how to introduce themselves to, and get to know, others. Teaching may focus on how the subjects may cue others that they have finished speaking or that they need to interrupt for a moment. They may have deficits in interpreting the nonverbal behaviours of others or even the verbal behaviours. The list goes on.

At a more advanced level, social skills training involves more complex chains of behaviours and skills. Social problem solving is one of these. Another is discrimination training, where and when certain social behaviours are acceptable and when and where they are not. Dating skills are important components for clients at certain stages of their lives.

Social skills can be grouped into three or four broad categories (McFall, 1982; Dodge, 1989). The first consists of those involved in correctly understanding the social situation and the actions of others. These are referred to as decoding skills. They include correctly interpreting verbal and nonverbal cues as well as understanding situation-specific demands. For example, can a person distinguish a malicious insult from a friendly jibe? Does a child recognise that approaching peers and initiating conversation in the playground will be welcomed but that in the classroom such behaviour will most probably be treated as an unwanted disturbance by peer and teacher alike?

The second group of skills comprises those involved in determining what responses are appropriate in particular situations. These skills require the ability to analyse situations, generate alternatives, evaluate probable outcomes and decide on responses. An example is recognising that one is angry and would like to punch another person, but deciding that it is not worth being charged with assault and therefore simply asking the person who has just run his car into the back of your two-day-old Jaguar for his insurance company's name.

The third group of skills consists of being able to enact the appropriate response once decided upon. For example, a person may decide that the best course of action is to initiate a conversation but be inhibited by anxiety or lack knowledge of how to do this. Likewise, another person may decide that an assertive response is required to a co-worker's criticism but be unsure of what to do to achieve that response.

Finally, people should monitor their own behaviour and alter it to suit the situational contingencies. One young man learned this when he insisted on 'being the man' and ordering a pizza in French in the French-speaking Canadian province of Quebec, even though his girlfriend was far more fluent in French. He had ample time to consider the wisdom of his actions as an irate girlfriend and he sat down to a pizza covered in green peas (he thought he had ordered green peppers!).

It is important to recognise that undesired behaviours may be due to the absence of more desirable responses in a person's repertoire of social skills. A child or an adult may be aggressive because of the lack of skills at any of the levels mentioned above. Interventions that are aimed only at decreasing the aggressive responses do little to enhance positive peer relationships unless prosocial behaviours are also taught (Kazdin, 1985).

Dodge (1989) has identified six stages involved in the assessment and treatment of problems in social competence:

- Identification of the socially incompetent person.
- Identifying the critical problematic social tasks for that person.
- Identifying situational factors related to the areas of incompetence.
- Improving cognitive skills related to the social skills involved.
- Improving behaviour in the problematic situations.
- Improving social standing among peers.

Social skills are certainly important but they are not the entire answer. An experience of one of us (Philip Barker) illustrates this.

A colleague in England – we will call her Ms Perkins – was conducting group sessions to teach social skills to delinquent boys in a correctional institution. Two recently released boys were one night detained by police, having been found in suspicious circumstances carrying housebreaking tools. They were taken to the police station and interviewed by the duty sergeant. He was struck by their courteous and respectful manner. They addressed him as 'Sir', stood obediently in front of his desk, and answered questions in an unusually polite way – at least for boys recently released. The sergeant was at first quite puzzled. Then an idea dawned on him.

'Have you been attending Ms Perkins' sessions at the Community Home?' he asked.

'Yes, we have,' they replied.

'So that explains it,' the sergeant responded.

At least they were polite criminals!

Chapter 13

Behavioural Approaches in Other Branches of Medicine

Many influences have worked together to bring about the marriage of behavioural techniques and the treatment of a wide variety of medical conditions (Gentry, 1984). There has been a decline in the proportion of patients presenting with infectious diseases as their main problem and a proportional increase in longevity. The reduced prevalence of infectious diseases combined with increased longevity have led to an increase in the relative prevalence of disorders caused or exacerbated by patients' own behaviour and by the collective lifestyle of the society around them. The best remedies for many of these problems are changes in behaviour.

Also relevant is the the reduction that has occurred in the mortality from many diseases. People with previously fatal conditions such as diabetes, cystic fibrosis, heart disease and muscular dystrophy, to name but a few, are living longer lives. But the increased longevity and decreased morbidity of these disorders are largely dependent on adherence to strict regimes of medication and lifestyle changes such as diet and exercise. Once again, the behaviour of the patient is a critical factor in determining the outcome of medical interventions. The physician now relies on the research of behaviourally orientated clinicians, if not their direct intervention, to bring adherence to acceptable levels.

It is important to distinguish behavioural medicine from behaviour therapy applied to medical problems. The term 'behavioural medicine' has been defined to include the integration of all branches of the mental health professions and social sciences as well as traditional biological medicine and related fields (Schwartz and Weiss, 1978). It also takes in all theoretical orientations. Nevertheless, it would be an understatement to say that behaviour therapy has made an enormous contribution to this fledgling field.

The ways in which behaviourally orientated therapists participate in the management of patients with medical diagnoses vary enormously, and there is also great untapped potential for further involvement. Behavioural interventions have been shown to be effective in understanding the epidemiology of some conditions, in preventing the occurrence, or ameliorating the consequences, of ischaemic heart disease, high blood pressure, cancer, obesity, asthma, urinary and fecal incontinence, migraine and irritable bowel syndrome (Blanchard, Schwartz, and Neff, 1988). They can also assist in brain injury rehabilitation and the management of chronic pain.

This involvement in medicine has led to a greater appreciation of the role of 'psychological' factors in 'biological' processes. To take cancer as an example, Derogatis (1986, page 632) states:

'With death no longer inevitable, oncologists increasingly recognise that motivation and behaviour are pivotal determinants of outcome across the entire spectrum of neoplastic diseases. The realisation has developed that the psychological status of the patient is as relevant to outcome as his or her biological state.'

The experience of pain is another example of how thinking has changed. At one time, conventional wisdom held that pain was a simple reflex: tissue was damaged, pain was perceived. However, psychophysiological studies have shown that pain is a complex phenomenon that is sometimes independent of tissue damage, and is based also on situational factors, prior learning, environmental contingencies and cognitive factors as well as physiological ones (Melzak, 1973). Jay, Elliott and Varni (1986, page 601) view pain as a 'trimodal interaction of behavioural, cognitive-affective, and physiological responses'. Furthermore, pain management may be greatly enhanced with the use of cognitive and behavioural interventions (Brena and Chapman, 1983). Many women now attend antenatal classes which teach skills, behaviours and ways of thinking which make childbirth pains more manageable, with measurable reductions in the reports of pain (Levanthal, Levanthal, Schacham, and Easterling, 1989).

Another important contributor to the marriage of behavioural approaches and medicine has been the success of the public health movement. The identification of sewage and refuse as breeding grounds for the bacteria that caused so much of the infectious diseases and plagues was merely a first step. The public health movement has brought about major changes in the behaviour of individuals and institutions – changes which have caused a marked improvement in the health of the general population. Increasingly, the example of this model and the recognition that many illnesses and chronic conditions can be prevented, or their onset delayed for many years, have led to a branch of behavioural medicine concerned with prevention. This includes all the research on smoking cessation, promoting no-smoking zones because of the danger of second-hand smoke, health and fitness promotion, lifestyle interventions, and weight loss and healthier diets which aim to reduce the risk of heart attack, stroke and cancer.

Behaviour therapy also provides a beneficial interface with medicine by ameliorating the effects of admission to hospital, stressful medical procedures and the incidental learning that interferes with medical treatment. It has been observed that some patients recover more quickly than others from surgery and other procedures and that this accelerated recovery seems to be related to different coping strategies, behaviours and cognitions. These can be taught to other patients, improving their recovery (Melamed *et al.*, 1982). Furthermore, recovery from disorders such as cancer seems to be linked in part to the behavioural and cognitive style of the patient (as is contracting cancer in the first place). Incidental learning can also cause anxiety and avoidance in patients who must undergo repeated distressing procedures such as daily burns dressing changes and chemotherapy for cancer. Interventions using behavioural techniques and principles can reverse, ameliorate or even prevent the occurrence of these reactions – reactions which otherwise can seriously compromise medical regimes (Kellerman and Varni, 1982).

Another area of interaction between medicine and behavioural approaches is in the treatment and rehabilitation of patients with brain injury. For example, behavioural techniques have been shown to be effective in reducing inappropriate verbalisations (Lewis *et al.*, 1988).

Behavioural conceptualisations and interventions can be of value at all stages of the disease process. Our understanding of the epidemiology of many diseases is being greatly enhanced through research which is identifying behavioural and cognitive risk factors for these diseases (Gentry, 1984). Having identified these risk factors, behavioural interventions are being developed to reduce the risk by altering these behaviours (see, for example, Leventhal *et al.*, 1984). The reduction of behavioural risk factors can also be accomplished at the community level (Farquhar *et al.*, 1984). Early research into the link between stress and illness showed the negative link between stress and illness. Stress increases the likelihood of physical illness developing. More recently, research has been directed at identifying the personal and environmental characteristics that buffer people from the debilitating effects of stress (Gentry and Kobasa, 1984). This clearly has implications for both treatment and prevention.

Once certain diseases have developed, behavioural treatments may be key components in the medical management plan (Agras, 1984; Russo and Varni, 1982). They may also be used to enhance the rate of compliance to the medical regime (Leventhal *et al.*, 1984; Masek and Jankel, 1982). Side effects may have a learned component or be amenable to management with behavioural interventions or both (Kellerman and Varni, 1982).

Treatment of disease can have three main outcomes: successful cure; no cure but ongoing management of an incurable condition or a condition resulting from treatment (for example, disfigurement due to surgical interventions such as amputation); or no cure progressing to a terminal phase. In the first instance – cure – behavioural interventions may help to prevent relapse (Leventhal *et al.*, 1984; Marlatt and Gordon, 1985). In the event that no cure can be found, behavioural interventions may be useful in enhancing the adaptation and coping of patients, their families or both when a chronic condition exists or the patient is in the terminal phase of the illness.

The patient as decision maker

One important contribution of the cognitive-behavioural approach to behavioural medicine has been the recognition that the patient is a decision maker. The patient is no longer viewed as a passive recipient of medical expertise but as an active evaluator of that information. Understanding how the patient makes decisions can enhance our ability to bring about healthy decisions and compliance to necessary medical regimes (Janis, 1984). Furthermore, the presence of two decision makers (doctor and patient) trying to arrive at a common solution to a problem (the patient's health concerns) makes this process transactional. This brings into play such behavioural factors as social perception, social judgment, assertiveness and communication skills.

To illustrate the above points, consider the following all-too-possible situation. A doctor recommends a certain medication to alleviate a particular condition and warns the patient of some possible side effects. The patient feels uneasy about this recommendation and is concerned that the side effects may occur. But the patient also remembers the crowded waiting room and the rapid-fire manner of questioning with which the doctor conducted the examination and judges the doctor to be too busy to deal with such 'petty' questions. Moreover, past experience has taught this patient that this doctor seems to interpret questions as challenges to his expertise and judgment. The patient – let us assume it is a man – lacking enough assertiveness to discuss his discomfort, merely nods his head and accepts the prescription slip. However, his unease remains and indeed grows as he repeats the doctor's list of possible side effects to himself. In the end the prescription remains unfilled and the patient avoids returning to the doctor's surgery out of embarrassment or goes to another doctor whom he does not inform about his visit to the first doctor. We must remember, though, that had the doctor not informed the patient of the possible side effects, and one or more of them had become evident, the patient's confidence in the doctor might well have been damaged. We therefore need to understand transactions of this sort, so that such dilemmas can be resolved.

Further reading

This chapter has provided only an outline of its subject. Useful sources of further information are: Russo and Varni (1982); Feuerstein *et al.* (1986); Lacks (1987); and Blanchard *et al.* (1988).

Chapter 14

Behaviour Therapy and Chronic Conditions

Therapy with chronic psychiatric patients

Great strides have been made in the last quarter century in understanding the biological causes of such debilitating conditions as schizophrenia and manic depressive – now more usually known as bipolar affective – disorders. Advances in our knowledge of the biology of these conditions have led to the use of treatments which have greatly improved many aspects of the functioning of these patients.

Major tranquillisers such as the phenothiazines and haloperidol can be of real benefit to those with schizophrenia, and lithium often effectively controls effectively the mood deviations of bipolar affective disorders. But these drugs do not reverse the social skill deficits many of these patients have, nor provide them with the skills of daily living that are essential if they are to cope outside the institutions in which they may have lived for years (Wallace *et al.*, 1985). Many of these patients need to be taught explicitly the behavioural and thinking skills they lack. This is where behavioural psychology has had a major impact.

Wallace and his colleagues (1985) have developed a programme of rehabilitating patients with chronic schizophrenia which focusses on three types of skills, in ten areas of functioning. The skills are:

- 'Sending skills' or the ability to perform behaviours.
- 'Receiving skills' or the skills necessary to understand and interpret situations accurately.
- 'Processing skills' or the skills needed to solve problems encountered in using the first two skills.

The ten areas of functioning have been developed into training modules and cover such areas as interpersonal skills, self-care skills and vocational skills.

The training programme is comprehensive and uses a wide variety of behavioural techniques in the assessment, treatment and evaluation of the skill deficits. These include, but are not limited to, behavioural interviews and checklists, role playing, behavioural contracting, reinforcement, modelling, shaping, videotape feedback and problem-solving training (Wallace *et al.*, 1985).

One of the two behavioural strategies most commonly employed with chronic psychiatric patients is the token economy (Hersen and Bellack, 1981). A token economy is a system whereby patients are provided with the necessities of life such as food, drink, shelter and medical care, but gain access to privileges, activities, goods and services by exchanging credits (called tokens) they have earned for performing desired behaviours.

The tokens can take many forms. They may be physical objects such as poker chips or more abstract forms such as points ('John, you earned ten points for greeting your visitor nicely') which are then recorded in a book or on a chart. These are 'secondary reinforcers'. They have no intrinsic power to motivate behaviour but do so because they can be exchanged for primary reinforcers – that is, reinforcers that are inherently motivating – at a later time. The latter are called 'back-up reinforcers'.

The range of back-up reinforcers should be wide, in order to prevent patients from becoming satiated when there are too few to choose from. This maintains the motivating qualities of the system. Furthermore, a balance must be maintained between making the back-up reinforcers too 'expensive' and having them too 'cheap', that is, easy to obtain. Either of these conditions would reduce the motivating qualities of the token economy. Response cost is usually worked into the system. Thus patients can lose tokens for inappropriate behaviour as well as earning them for appropriate actions.

A major advantage of the token economy is its similarity to the more general economy of the noninstitutional society. People earn tokens (money) for performing desired behaviours (work) which are exchanged for a wide range of back-up reinforcers (food, clothing, material goods, recreation), and when a sufficiently undesirable behaviour is detected (for example, breaking road traffic laws) a fine of so many tokens (money) is levied. Like people managing their money, psychiatric patients must manage their tokens in order to obtain some of the more desirable and therefore more expensive back-up reinforcers. This offers the opportunity to learn and practise such skills as budgeting and long-term planning.

A token economy's effectiveness is generally enhanced if it is tailored to the individual needs of the patients, for each of whom unique behaviours are the targets. So one patient may receive bonus points on a DRO schedule for not being aggressive (so many tokens for each unit of time such as an hour, a half day or some other interval, during which the patient is not aggressive). Another might receive bonus points for attending a job-training programme.

Token economies have been shown to be successful in improving the functioning level of the patients involved. They are superior to milieu therapy or pharmacotherapy alone in improving both ward behaviour and relapse rates. Yet there is no guarantee that behaviour learned in a hospital ward will generalise to the community and be maintained after discharge (Hersen and Bellack, 1981).

The other behavioural intervention commonly used with chronic psychiatric patients is social skills training. Difficulty in coping with the social environment is probably the most common problem these patients face, regardless of their diagnoses. The critical nature of these skills is demonstrated by the fact that preadmisson social competence (as measured by marital, work and school histories) is the best predictor of posthospital adjustment (Hersen and Bellack, 1981). There is often a need for teaching in all three major skill areas. These are:

- Verbal content.
- Paralinguistic aspects of speech such as tone, pace and volume.
- Nonverbal communication such as posture, facial expression and gestures.

Patients must also develop an appreciation of the situational nature of social skills, that a correct behaviour in one situation is incorrect in another. For example, 'Have a nice day!' may be a perfectly good way to finish off many a social encounter but is unsuitable at the end of a funeral. As we have seen earlier, we must also determine whether the lack of skill displayed by a patient is a result of that person never having learned the skill (skill deficit), or whether the skill was learned but is not performed due to lack of reinforcement or practice, or because of the interference of incompatible behaviours (performance deficit).

Research shows that patients do make gains in social functioning through social skills training (Hersen and Bellack, 1981).

Treatments which are effective with outpatients can frequently be used effectively also with inpatients. Thus the addition of cognitive therapy to standard inpatient treatment of depression results in a better long-term outcome (Miller *et al.*, 1989).

Behavioural approaches and the developmentally disabled

Behaviour therapy has a long history of assisting in the management of patients with intellectual and physical developmental delays. Its impact has been to improve the quality of life for these patients by helping develop more effective means of educating them and enhancing their skill development.

An example of the use of behavioural interventions is provided by the report of the reduction of disruptive and stereotyped behaviours of three severely retarded and multihandicapped pre-school children through the use of behavioural assessment, DRO schedules and generalisation (Sisson, Van Hasselt, Hersen and Aurand, 1988). There is also evidence that behaviour therapy effects are observable by other children and make developmentally handicapped children (in the study in question these were autistic) more acceptable and approachable (Runco and Schreibman, 1988).

Children with varying degrees of mental retardation have long been the focus of behavioural interventions. Crnic and Reid (1989, page 247), suggest that:

'Perhaps no other childhood disorder has contributed as much to the development of behavioral interventions with children as has mental retardation.'

As many as 50 per cent of children with mental retardation have additionable diagnosable psychiatric illnesses (Jacobsen, 1982). The types of problems mentally retarded children present with range from specific academic, social and vocational problems to 'complex and extensive response deficiencies, such as a lack of interpersonal relatedness' (Crnic and Reid, 1989, page 252).

Behavioural treatments with the mentally handicapped have to date emphasised the use of operant techniques. These techniques have enjoyed great success in bringing about positive changes in the behaviour of these children, but this success has been marred by poor generalisation and maintenance of the gains. While applied behaviour analysis has been the most common approach to date, therapists are broadening the range of behavioural interventions they use. Of particular note is the increased use of cognitive-behavioural techniques and behavioural family therapy (Crnic and Reid, 1989).

The latter approach reflects the growing trend in behavioural circles to think in ecological or systemic terms. This is particularly true in the field of mental retardation. Therapists have recognised that the affective, behavioural and cognitive status of the mentally retarded child has a profound impact on the functioning of the family. Reciprocally, the degree to which the family is functioning well or poorly has its impact on the mentally retarded child and his or her development (Crnic and Reid, 1989).

Another current development in behavioural theory is also having its effect on the treatment of the mentally retarded. This is the concept of developmental psychopathology (Cicchetti, 1984). This concept, that children's adaptive and behavioural problems must be considered in the light of their developmental status, has obvious implications for treatment of the mentally retarded. There is a need to match the interventions to the children's abilities (Crnic and Reid, 1989). Thus some mentally retarded children can benefit from certain types of cognitive intervention while others cannot.

There is another trend which is taking the behavioural treatment of mentally retarded children away from traditional behavioural analysis. Behavioural analysis is a 'molecular' approach to behaviour change. It isolates one or a few behaviours which are then studied intensively and modified directly by changing the conditions which maintain the behaviour. This ignores the impact that changing these few behaviours has on other systems of which they are part. There is a need to monitor other behaviours and other parts of the system for change as one modifies the target behaviour. It does the mentally retarded child no good to lessen one problematic behaviour only to have another equally or more serious behaviour problem emerge or to have, as the cost of successfully modifying the behaviour, an increase in the level of dysfunction in the family (Crnic and Reid, 1989).

(This last observation, of course, applies also to interventions with children and adults who have other behavioural difficulties and are not developmentally delayed.)

The autistic child

Behaviour therapy may be particularly applicable to autistic children and adults, who usually have severely impaired verbal communication skills, so that the 'talking therapies' are relatively ineffective. Indeed, by systematically teaching specific motor skills and demonstrating behaviourally that these children are able to interact with their environments and learn, behaviourists have shown that these children are more capable than they are often thought to be.

Behavioural approaches do seem to be the treatment of choice for autistic children. The primary form of intervention remains operant conditioning and imitative learning. Newsom and Rincover (1989, page 293), in discussing prognosis, note that:

'The main factor in determining outcome was whether or not the child received intensive behaviourally oriented intervention programs before the age of five years.'

The trend towards matching children's abilities with treatment goals is also reflected in the approach used in treating autistic children. Newsom and Rincover (1989) report that two groups of autistic children are emerging, each requiring particular treatment approaches. The major factor which distinguishes these two groups is their intellectual ability, although other factors are also relevant. Autistic children who are severely or profoundly retarded have a much poorer prognosis. For these children, the most appropriate goal is for them to acquire behaviours which will make their lives easier and allow as much independence as possible. In contrast, autistic children in the normal or mildly retarded ranges of intelligence should receive highly intensive 'total push' programmes in order to 'take maximum advantage of the plasticity of neurological and behavioural processess early in life' (Newsom and Rincover, 1989, page 294).

Autistic children are taught, especially in the initial stages, using the most basic of operant techniques. They are taught the necessary prerequisite skills that allow later learning. This begins with conditioning them to attend to the task at hand, starting with attending to the teacher. In addition, the frequency of behaviours disruptive to the learning process is reduced. One of the more effective ways of doing this is to teach the child to comply to requests. Studies have shown compliance and disruptive behaviours to be mutually exclusive response categories. As the strength of the compliance responses increases, the disruptive behaviours decrease (Newsom and Rincover, 1989).

An area in which behaviour therapy has been quite effective is in the reduction or even elimination of self-mutilating behaviours. At first, these gains were obtained at the cost of considerable controversy, since the methods used were generally contingent punishment, often in the form of electric shock. Today, however, behaviour therapists often obtain the same results using non-aversive techniques. It has been found that many of these behaviours can be reduced using reinforcement. For this to be achieved a correct analysis of the behaviour must first be achieved. Then suitable schedules of reinforcement (such as DRO and DRL) are used to increase incompatible behaviours, or appropriate alternative skills are taught to achieve the goals which the disquieting behaviour has achieved (LaVigna and Donnellan, 1987).

The place of aversive techniques in the treatment of autistic children has long been the subject of controversy. The debate continues to this day. The trend is clearly towards a reduction in the use of these techniques. Most therapists and governing bodies recognise that they should be used only as a last resort, after less intrusive methods have been tried and have failed. A major advantage of the ongoing debate has been to increase efforts to develop nonaversive ways of dealing with disruptive and dangerous behaviours. The therapist treating an autistic child in the 1990s has many more techniques available to try before resorting to aversive procedures than did those therapists who first began applying behavioural techniques to this population.

The trend towards doing more work with families, seen in other areas of behaviour therapy, has also been evident in the treatment of autistic children. Much attention has been given to training parents in the appropriate management of their autistic children. This has been found to be effective in enhancing the functioning both of autistic children and of their families. Several models of service delivery have been effective in this regard (Harris, 1989).

Chapter 15

Philosophical and Ethical Issues in Behaviour Therapy

Therapy methods based on learning theory have been subjected to many challenges based on ethical considerations. In this chapter we will discuss some of the major areas of challenge.

The issue of control

Learning theory seeks to bring psychology into the scientific community through the application of scientific methods to psychological phenomena. Among other things, the goals of the scientific method include the prediction and control of the phenomenon being studied. It is this latter goal that has created some controversy. For psychologists to attempt to *control*, rather than just to study, behaviour was considered by some a dangerous approach.

One of the key ethical questions behaviour therapists must face is that of who shall decide which behaviours in which persons will be changed and by whom. There is nothing inherent in learning theory that can answer such questions. It provides us with no standards of what is healthy or optimal functioning. It merely describes the mechanisms by which behaviours are learned and maintained, and makes the assumption that the mechanisms for learning behaviours deemed 'bad' are the same as the mechanisms for behaviours deemed 'good'.

Learning theory, upon which behaviour therapy is based, is the scientific study of a specific aspect of nature, namely, how organisms learn to behave. In general, the search for 'natural' moral laws has been unsuccessful. Nature is amoral. As Kant has pointed out (in MacIntyre, 1966), we must look for our moral standards outside the realm of nature.

'Good' is a relative term. It is a judgment passed upon something or action, not an inherent quality of that thing or action. As McIntyre (1966) paraphrases Aristotle:

'Good is defined at the outset in terms of the goal, purpose, or aim to which something or somebody moves. To call something good is to say that it is under certain conditions sought or aimed at. There are numerous activities, numerous aims, and hence numerous goods.'

Behaviour therapy itself is amoral. Its application may be judged beneficial or harmful but the approach itself is neither one nor the other. It is much like any other tool. Take, for example, an axe. An axe has many useful purposes. It may also be used to kill. However, we do not judge axes to be evil and banish their use because on occasion they are used to kill. Imagine where our social and technological evolution would be today if the original stone axes had been banned because they could kill. But we must look at another theoretical/philosophical issue in conjunction with the issue of control, in order to understand fully this dilemma.

Determinism versus free will

Another major ethical objection to the very premises of learning theory lies in the issue of determinism versus free will (Craighead, Kazdin and Mahoney, 1981). One premise of science, and therefore of a scientific psychology, is that events are caused; they are determined by the actions that precede them. This seems to eliminate the concept of free will that is inherent in most moral codes and is a central concept of law.

At least in part, the trouble lies in the difficulty which defining free will presents. Is it that people are to be held accountable for their actions and must consider the consequences before they act, or is it that human action is independent of causation and therefore independent of context? The former position is not incompatible with learning theory as we will see shortly. The latter is a very hard position to maintain – that behaviour is independent of its consequences and independent of the context in which it occurs.

It is important to distinguish the concept of determinism, upon which learning theory is based, from the concept of predeterminism (Craighead *et al.*, 1981). Determinism says that events are caused and can be understood by examining the preceding events in a causal chain. Thus A causes B.

Predeterminism states that all events are determined according to an unalterable plan. A will cause B no matter what. Determinism maintains that the codes of conduct are part of the social environment and therefore part of the causal chain. Behaviour may be determined, at least in part, by the anticipation of divine, legal or social reward or censure. Predeterminism makes these moral codes incidental to anything, merely another part of the 'plan' or, as the judge said in response to the defendant who stated he could not be held accountable for his actions since all events were predetermined: 'In that case, it is also predetermined that I must sentence you to five years in jail.'

In other words, holding people responsible for their behaviour is an important environmental variable because it makes known the contingencies which apply for the behaviour in question (Craighead *et al.*, 1981). The demonstration of purposeful action in the absence of feedback from the environment would provide a much stronger case for free will – action not based on environmental consequences.

The basic question behaviour therapy faces is that of who is to be held accountable to whom. Learning theory seems to provide the technology that allows the creation of a totalitarian state. This is not a necessary conclusion, however, because it ignores the concepts of reciprocity and countercontrol.

Reciprocity

A major problem lies in the way learning theory has often been presented. A behaviour is performed by an experimental animal and then an experimenter administers a reward, thus gaining control of the animal's behaviour. When a person is substituted for the experimental animal, an unpleasant image is invoked – not unlike that of a puppet and puppeteer. But this presentation fails to take into account the systemic aspect of the interaction.

The above point was well illustrated by a cartoon showing two rats in a learning experiment in which they press a bar to obtain food. One rat says to the other: 'Boy, have I got this guy well trained. Every time I press this bar, he gives me food.' By performing the desired behaviour, repeatedly pressing the bar, the rat was rewarding the experimenter. Who was controlling whom? Control is not a one-way street. It is reciprocal (Craighead *et al.*, 1981). Of course, any parent trying to control a child could have told you that!

The above is not such a facetious statement. A child misbehaves and is spanked by a parent. The child stops the problem behaviour. The child does something else wrong. The parent spanks again and the behaviour stops again. Who is controlling whom? Does the parent spank the child because she has the power and can control the child through punishment by application, or does the child control the parent by reinforcing the parent's spanking with the cessation of the problem behaviour (negative reinforcement)? Each of the above processes is occurring. Each is controlling the other. (Wouldn't the child like to know that!)

Similarly, if a child repeats a positive action, such as telling the parent he has to go 'potty', when the parent gives the child a sweet for doing so, who is rewarding whom? Each is rewarding and controlling the other. The parent reinforces the reporting with the treat, and the child reinforces the giving of the treat with the desired report of a full bowel.

Countercontrol

Countercontrol is another observed phenomenon that argues against the thesis that learning theory is the technology of totalitarianism (Craighead *et al.*, 1981). It consists of intentionally not making a predictable response in order to elude control. Not being controlled by the person trying to administer the consequences is the reward which maintains the behaviour. We refer to it as rebelliousness. It is seen in civil disobedience; in teenagers who refuse to 'recognise the rules'; and in prisoners of war and political prisoners who sometimes suffer tremendous personal costs in order to avoid giving in to the control of their captors. Countercontrol is itself a determined response, generated from the learning history of the subjects and the current contexts in which they find themselves.

Behaviour therapy and power

The real question we face concerns power. Power can be defined as the relative control over the distribution of rewards and punishments and the ability to deliver them contingently (Martin and Pear, 1983). Who controls the rewards and punishments, and to what extent, become central questions and underlie political philosophies. Democracy attempts to deal with the issue of who controls the rewards and punishments through an element of reciprocal control, while the *theory* underlying communist and socialist philosophies is to prevent the concentration of reinforcers and punishments in the hands of too few people (Martin and Pear, 1981).

In western democracies, the problem of who controls the power is dealt with through division of power and reciprocal control. Different countries divide the powers differently. The creation of laws is usually separated from the interpretation and administration of 'justice'. Often, more than one branch or body of government must approve a proposed law (a statement of contingencies) for it to become effective. Other branches of government, or agencies, are responsible for administering the law (the ability not only to control rewards and punishments but deliver them contingently). There are often different levels of government responsible for different jurisdictions.

Reciprocal control is exercised through the existence of laws which provide rewards for certain actions. Some examples are government grants to performing arts groups, subsidies to farmers to grow certain crops, interest-free loans to companies who locate in areas of low employment and tax reductions for charitable donations. The government has the right to punish certain other actions, through increasing taxes (in order to discourage the use of tobacco and alcohol, for example), the levying of fines (response cost) and extended time out (jail!).

Citizens in turn can reward and punish their elected representatives through their votes, through donations to candidates' campaign funds, by volunteering their time and by writing letters indicating their support of or objection to different issues (which will indicate to the politician a future contingency, the likelihood of re-election). The right of free speech is essential to this process as it allows objections or support to be raised to the manner in which power is being used.

In democracies which also endorse capitalism to a greater or lesser extent, there is the added philosophical position that supply and demand should dictate the distribution of power. The concept is that people vote for – that is, reward with their money – those people who provide the goods and services they desire. In part, this includes the government, although in this case the money is collected as taxes and people demonstrate their consent, or lack of it, on election day.

According to communist philosophy, control of resources and the means of production is the key to control over rewards and punishments. The concern is that under capitalistic systems this power gets concentrated into the hands of too few people. Hence, power should rest with all the people as represented by government.

The negative reactions to potentially effective technologies for behaviour change are due in part to the past abuses of power that lace our collective histories. Thus people tend to reject any system of control. The misuse of power can itself be considered a behaviour problem amenable to behaviour change techniques (Martin and Pear, 1983). We leave it to our readers to form their own opinions as to how the different political systems have dealt with the potential abuse of power.

'Wants' versus contingencies

A concept of free will is that we do things because we 'want' to do them, not because of environmental contingencies. But this position overlooks the point that our wants, desires and hopes are themselves determined by our learning histories and our expectations of the rewards and punishments which will ensue if we engage or fail to engage in particular behaviours (Craighead *et al.*, 1981). This is the very premise of advertising – that desires can be learned.

It is sometimes maintained that any attempt at behaviour change is unethical. If this position were accepted, however, it would disqualify the actions of all who try to help – including teachers, ministers of religion, governments and parents, to say nothing of therapists (Martin and Pear, 1981).

Behaviour therapy and humanism

Another objection sometimes raised to behaviour therapy is that behavioural theories are dehumanising. They present an overly simplistic and mechanical view of people and imply that we are not in control of our own behaviour. Behavioural techniques can, however, be used to encourage creativity, to expand the range of behaviours available to people, to provide people with the means to achieve the goals they have set for themselves and indeed, by understanding the process by which their behaviour is learned and maintained, give them more self-control than they ever had before. This is because now they can engineer their own environments to support the behaviours they desire.

In other words, rather than dehumanising, behavioural techniques may help us to be more effectively human (Craighead *et al.*, 1981). Indeed, behavioural techniques can be used to help us with the process of self-actualisation.

The issue of 'freedom'

When we speak of freedom, we usually consider this to be the maximisation of the number of alternative actions available to us in any given situation, and the ability to choose freely among the available alternatives. But it is not hard to see that behavioural freedom is the result of an interaction between people and their environment. It requires that we be able to execute the behaviour effectively and that the environment allows that action to be taken.

Choice means that we consider the potential consequences of each of the alternatives available to us; we are then likely to choose the option that maximises our rewards and minimises our costs. Our behavioural freedom can be increased by increasing our skills, decreasing the restrictions presented by the environment, and minimising the costs of any potential action. Maximum freedom would exist (and probably maximum indecision also) when all options are available, all actions can be carried out by the person, and there is no cost for any action, and equal reward.

Consider a man confined to a wheelchair. He may be an expert computer programmer (that is, he can effectively execute this skill) but his behavioural freedom is restricted to working for those companies whose buildings are wheelchair accessible. Likewise, his recreational options are restricted to places and activities that accommodate a wheelchair.

On the other hand, consider a person who is able bodied but illiterate. This person has limited behavioural freedom because of the skill deficit, not because of the immediate environment. The work and recreational options open to this person are restricted to those not requiring reading.

Consider a third person. This is an able-bodied and literate black man living in South Africa. Here his behavioural freedom, for example, concerning where he may live, is restricted by potentially severe sanctions (official and unofficial). The cost of enacting many options is simply too high for most to pay. (Note also the phenomenon of countercontrol, however, whereby many *are* willing to pay the price to establish behavioural freedom.)

In order to maximise behavioural freedom for the greatest possible number of people within a society, there must be agreed limits to the scope of behavioural freedom. Without these limits, behavioural freedoms are quickly lost for the majority as power accummulates in the hands of a few. These few then usually use their unrestricted behavioural freedom to place limits on the behavioural freedoms of the rest.

Therapists are bound by the same restrictions as their clients in this regard. To cite an obvious example, it is not a viable option for a therapist to teach a client an effective way to kill a spouse as a way of maximising behavioural freedom in dealing with marital conflict. However, within the strictures of such limits behavioural therapists should be committed to maximising their clients' behavioural freedoms. We believe that most are. Indeed, we believe the commitment should be there in therapists of all theoretical orientations, and generally it is.

In choosing therapeutic interventions, behaviour therapists are guided by the principle of maximising behavioural freedom. It is called the 'least restrictive alternative' doctrine and is established in the ethical standards of the Association for the Advancement of Behaviour Therapy (AABT).

The least restrictive doctrine is in part established by legal precedence and process (Craighead *et al.*, 1981). This has implications for treatment programmes in institutions, since courts have defined as rights many potential rewards that were previously deemed to be privileges (Craighead *et al.*, 1981). Basically, this doctrine states that the therapeutic technique chosen (regardless of theoretical orientation) must be the one with the least cost to the client. Cost in this case is not only monetary, but covers distress, physical or emotional pain and restriction of rights. In behavioural terms, this means that skill building, positive reinforcement programmes and extinction should be used before milder forms of punishment such as response cost. Response cost should be used before any programme that uses stimuli likely to be aversive to the client (such as electric shock or nausea-inducing drugs – which are sometimes used to treat paraphilias and addictions).

The above considerations also mean that outpatient treatment must be attempted before the client is placed in a restricted environment except where there is a clear danger to the client or to others. The principle of the 'least restrictive option' is established in many institutions where behaviour therapy is practised, through the use of guidelines which state that less restrictive and less aversive methods must be used before more restrictive and more aversive. In addition, such guidelines usually identify which techniques are considered less restrictive than others. The Alberta Children's Hospital, where we both work, has such guidelines. Included in those guidelines are the concepts of increased monitoring and consultation as the level of restriction increases. Therapy programmes must also return to lower levels of behavioural restriction as quickly as possible.

Accountability

The right of a client or the client's legal guardian to hold the therapist accountable also provides a safeguard against the misuse of behavioural techniques. Behaviour therapists are not immune from the laws of learning. Hence, they are likely to persist in those therapeutic behaviours which are effective, and are acceptable to their clients and those responsible for their clients; and to avoid the sanctions of their employers (if they are employed in an agency or institution), of their professional association or licensing body, and of the legal system. Therapists can be rewarded and punished for their behaviour, just as clients can be. They can be hired or fired, given awards or fines, allowed to continue to practise or be dismissed from their profession, and they may even be placed in jail.

Freedom through knowledge

The notion that knowledge of how we acquire behaviours and how they persist should not be used in a therapeutic context is hard to understand. There is overwhelming research evidence for the principles of learning discussed earlier in this book. As yet, the knowledge is incomplete and it may yet be shown that cognitive-behavioural principles cannot provide a complete explanation of human functioning. On the other hand, if learning theory does explain all or even a significant portion of how behaviour is acquired and maintained, is it not better that these processes be understood and applied logically and beneficially, rather than capriciously and even maliciously? Should parents who control their children through punishment and negative reinforcement, and who in turn are controlled by their children in similar fashion to the point where everyone is miserable, be denied the knowledge we have of learning principles so as to avoid any hint of conscious control? (These people, we must realise, are usually unaware of these patterns in their behaviour.)

To take a wider view, should only a few people in power understand these principles or should they be openly studied and in the hands of all? It is easier to avoid being manipulated by the techniques if one understands and recognises them.

This leads us to the next protective safeguard for clients. The client or the guardian of the client should be fully informed of the treatment plan, the target behaviours and the methods to be used to bring about the changes, before treatment begins.

The use of aversive techniques

Special attention needs to be paid to the use of aversive techiques in treatment. Even within behaviour therapy journals and meetings, there is considerable controversy over the place, if any, of aversive techniques in therapy. The use of step procedures as explained earlier in this chapter – that one uses aversive techniques only after less aversive techniques have been shown to be ineffective – and subject to informed consent being given and the patient's rights considered (Craighead *et al.*, 1981) lessens the controversy somewhat. There also must be adequate training for all those using these techniques. Proper supervision is also essential as therapy staff use aversive procedures, together with a system of checks and balances and proper accountability (Martin and Pear, 1981). The question – whether aversive techniques are ever justified – of course remains. At present we do not have a definitive answer to this.

When objections are arised to aversive techniques, we need to consider whether the objection is to techniques which are subjectively aversive (distasteful to the observer), or functionally aversive – that is to say that when they are presented contingent upon the performance of a behaviour, the likelihood that behaviour will occur again is reduced (Bernstein, 1989). Bernstein notes that the objection to the use of aversive methods applies to the prior definition (the subjective one), not the latter. This then becomes a matter not of science but of values. It is a scientific issue whether a therapy works.

It is a personal and social issue which techniques should be used and which should not. The role that a science of behaviour can play is to determine what are the acceptable standards in the views of (a) the clients, (b) the general public and (c) therapists. The debate over the use of nuclear energy illustrates a similar dilemma. Science can determine the potential uses of power contained in the atom, but society must determine whether it should be used at all.

Griffith and Spreat (1989) couch the argument somewhat differently. To these two authors it is the issue of an outright ban versus expert professional judgment. They point out that no one is advocating the routine use of aversive procedures but rather the retention of the option of using aversive procedures where expert clinical judgment deems them necessary. In part, the controversy concerns whether or not there are sufficiently effective nonaversive techniques that eliminate the need for aversive techniques. Some authors claim there are (LaVigna and Donnellan, 1986), while others claim there is insufficient evidence for adequate alternatives (Axelrod, 1987).

Professional issues

The final issue in the debate is the matter of determining the competence of the persons administering the treatment. Griffith and Spreat (1989) maintain that a major problem is that the technology of behavioural analysis is too often used by underqualified practitioners. This is an important matter but it addresses a somewhat different issue, namely that of whether the mental health professions and institutions are adequately regulating themselves.

In short, behaviour therapists need to be mindful of the ethical principles that guide all mental health practitioners. They need to be competent, knowledgeable practitioners who maintain their knowledge and skills through reading and continuing education. They need to exercise sound clinical judgment, based on empirical data. They need to respect their clients and their clients' rights to the best possible treatment, which is the least restrictive and intrusive. They must ensure that fully informed consent has been given for the treatment being used. They need to keep in mind the norms and laws of the wider society except when those norms and laws are unfairly restrictive of their clients' behavioural freedom (as in the case where racial, religious or other discrimination is practised – be it official or unofficial). They need to guard against the abuse of the knowledge they possess by seeking consultation whenever necessary and by participating in peer review programmes. The specific restrictions on the use of particular techniques will be determined empirically. This will be achieved by the demonstration of which are the most effective techniques; and also by society, which will ultimately determine, through public opinion and by the enactment of laws, whether the techniques can be used.

Chapter 16

The Current Status and Future of Behaviour Therapy

Behaviour therapy, especially its cognitive variant, is a relative newcomer among the psychotherapies. Along with family therapy, it has only gained acceptance since World War II, indeed mainly in the last 20 to 30 years. Its acceptance has often been grudging, at least among some sections of the mental health professions.

Why has the acceptance of behaviour therapy come so slowly, and at least three decades after Pavlov's death? Why the reluctance to accept the behavioural approach to the treatment of behavioural and emotional problems? And how far is this reluctance disappearing? Will the decades ahead see behaviour therapy continuing to play an increasing part in our treatment programmes? Of course, only time will provide the answers to these questions but this chapter will speculate on behaviour therapy's future.

An important factor in the reluctance which many mental health professionals have displayed in embracing behavioural approaches has been the long-held view of the predominantly unconscious origin of people's problems. North American psychiatry in particular accepted the Freudian view of psychiatric disorders in a largely unquestioning way for several decades. 'Dynamic psychotherapy' – that is, therapy designed to explore and deal with unconscious conflicts and problems – was seen as the psychotherapy of choice in most clinical situations. Therapists sought always to discover the unconscious roots of the disorders they were treating. Only then was true cure possible.

Behaviour therapy challenged this view. It ignored – or even discounted – the postulated 'unconscious' origins of symptoms. Instead, it stated that the symptom *is* the problem. All the therapist need do is discover what are the contingencies maintaining the behaviour, make appropriate alterations in these, and the 'problem' is solved. The above approach worked well with certain disorders, for example, specific phobias, but it was less successful with more complex disorders and it did not address problems in thinking or feeling. It was still possible for the psychodynamically inclined to take the view that, while perhaps a few symptoms such as isolated phobias might be due to special learning experiences, the approach was not applicable to the generality of psychiatric disorders.

Until quite recently, this was the status of behaviour therapy in the eyes of many mental health professionals. The behavioural approach was peripheral to the mainstream of psychiatry.

The advent of cognitive-behavioural approaches, and the increasing willingness of behaviour therapists to work on the thought processes and reported inner lives of their patients, were significant developments. No longer were the efforts of behaviourists seen as applicable only to a few clearcut, objectively observable symptoms, but they were proposing means of changing the ways people think. In other words, the worlds of the dynamic psychotherapist and of the behaviour therapist were merging, at least in so far as they both dealt with thoughts and feelings.

Another important development was the increasing acceptance by most behaviour therapists of the limitations of their methods. At first, many of them tended to take the view that all behaviour was learned. The learning experiences of all of us had only to be made more appropriate and we could be perfectly adjusted human beings. At the same time, however, the work of geneticists and neurobiologists revealed that other factors play their part in conditions such as schizophrenia and major affective disorders. Psychopharmacological agents are effective in certain conditions. The fact that other factors operate does not, of course, mean that patients' conditions cannot be ameliorated, or ever cured, by behavioural means, but it does tell us that these disorders are not just due to deviant learning in otherwise normal individuals. It also suggests that other, perhaps physical or pharmacological, treatments may also be of value.

It has also become clear that we are all born with different temperamental characteristics. The work of Chess and Thomas (1984) has shown just how important our temperamental endowment is, and how the 'fit' between parents' temperaments and the temperaments of their children can help determine whether or not their children develop behavioural problems.

Clashes between parents and their children – common problems in the practices of child psychiatrists and psychologists – may be due primarily to temperamental incompatibility rather than to deviant learning experiences. Here again, however, behavioural approaches may still have important roles to play in therapy.

All the above points have increasingly been accepted by practitioners of behaviour therapy, who have come to see the use of behavioural treatment methods as often having their most effective application as part of larger treatment plans which often involve other methods. It has also become evident (at least to most therapists) that no one treatment approach can provide the answer to all human problems.

Professional differences

Behaviour therapy has been developed almost exclusively by psychologists. This has probably slowed the acceptance of behavioural methods by many psychiatrists and medically orientated treatment facilities. These methods have not, until quite recently, been regarded as part of the mainstream of psychiatry. This is changing, as psychologists become integral members of mental health teams, and the scientific data supporting their claims of valuable therapeutic gains from their methods become less and less deniable.

We believe it is significant that this book is written jointly by a psychologist and a psychiatrist. Moreover, we are clinical colleagues who work together in a hospital treating severely disturbed children and their families. It would be inconceivable that either of us could function in the way we see as optimal, in this work, if we were unable to pool our respective skills and areas of expertise. This close relationship between the disciplines of psychology and psychiatry is probably quite typical of that which is taking place in many settings in which psychiatric disorders are treated. We certainly hope so, as the benefits to patients are clear to us.

The scientific approach

Something which has characterised the behavioural approach from the start has been the careful way most psychologists – the professional group which has pioneered these treatment methods – have collected their data and subjected them to statistical analysis. It is safe to say that there are more hard data on the effectiveness of behavioural methods than there are on any other type of psychotherapy. It is hard for anyone with a scientific bent to deny many of the claims of behaviourists. Not only does this help these methods to gain general acceptance, but it also points the way to the better scientific validation of other forms of psychotherapy.

The systems view

One of the most important developments of the last two or three decades has been the acceptance by many therapists of the systems view of human behaviour. This is a major development. Until quite recently psychotherapy, for most therapists, was a matter of treating individuals for their own particular problems. This applied even to group therapies. Although patients might be treated in groups, this was seen as an alternative way of helping them with their individual problems. Group members might gain from the input of other members of the group and thus learn something that would be of value to them in their own personal recoveries.

Systems theory sees human problems as being often – some would even say always – embedded in the functioning of the social systems of which the afflicted persons are part. This is the basis of most family therapy approaches. We are not islands. We are constantly interacting with those around us. These interactions are immensely complex, and applying behavioural techniques to their analysis and to making them more functional represent major challenges. We have seen, however, in earlier chapters, that this challenge is being taken up by many behaviour therapists. Even ten years ago behavioural methods were being widely used as a major means of treating marital couples (Jacobson and Margolin, 1979). Modifying the methods for use in more complex systems, involving larger numbers of people, is a major challenge facing behaviour therapists today.

While there is no reason to suppose that the laws of learning theory apply any less to the interactions of people in family and other groups than they do in one-to-one situations, applying behavioural techniques in these situations is more challenging. The work of Patterson and his colleagues with the families of children with behaviour problems (Patterson, 1982) has, however, shown us various ways of overcoming some of the difficulties these situations present.

The future

Behavioural methods of promoting changes in human behaviour are surely here to stay. Moreover, they have application in fields much wider than the treatment of mental health problems. They may be used in prevention and in improving the functioning of people in their everyday lives. Many of those who use such methods suffer from no psychiatric or other disorder. They simply wish to improve their functioning in social, occupational, athletic or other areas of their lives. Yet achieving such improvements may lessen their chance of getting into difficulty and, perhaps, of developing a psychiatric disorder when faced with stresses with which they are unprepared to deal.

When we consider the treatment of established behavioural and psychiatric disorders, a place for behavioural approaches among the methods regularly used seems assured. Human beings, of any age and at any stage of life, are learning, developing organisms. Some learn more readily than others, and indeed it is many of those who have difficulty in learning that are most prone to develop problem behaviours – behaviours which may be regarded as manifestations of mental illness. This suggests that the learning situations each of our patients experiences or, to put it in more 'behavioural' terms, the contingencies that are operating, need always to be taken into account.

An illustration of the above point is provided by the work that has been done on expressed emotion in the families of schizophrenic patients (Leff and Vaughn, 1985). Few would any longer maintain that schizophrenia is caused by the family environment in which those afflicted live (as some of the early family therapists did). Yet it does appear that the environment into which schizophrenic patients are discharged plays an important part in determining whether relapse will occur. A high level of 'expressed emotion' (Leff and Vaughn, 1985) within the family in which the schizophrenic person goes to live appears to increase the probability of relapse.

Considerations such as the above suggest that, in our clinical work, we cannot afford to overlook the environmental contingencies to which our patients are exposed. The behaviour therapist, or the behavioural analyst, is best equipped to become the clinical team's expert in this area.

It is interesting to consider how the role played by psychologists in multidisciplinary mental health teams has changed over the years. Psychologists were mainly responsible for the development of intelligence and other psychometric tests. In the traditional 'child guidance team', the psychologist was the member who carried out those tests that were considered necessary when a child presented for treatment. Intelligence tests were foremost among those administered, though tests of educational attainment were also widely used, and personality tests to a lesser degree. Nowadays much less attention is paid to intelligence tests results. They have their place but they are no longer used in the routine way they were.

The decline in the emphasis on test administration has coincided with an increase in the attention paid to environmental contingencies in clinical work. Routine psychometric testing is no longer seen as necessary, but perhaps routine assessment of every psychiatric patient's past and, especially, present learning situation and cognitions will soon be regarded as essential. Intelligence testing investigates simply the ability of the subject to perform certain cognitive tasks and compares this with that of the population on which the test has been standardised. More important in many cases, we now realise, is the content of the person's cognitions. This content may well be a more important determinant of behaviour than the person's thinking capacity.

What of the future of behaviour therapy in other fields? Perhaps the term *behavioural analysis* or *the behavioural approach* are to be preferred to terms which feature the word *therapy*. The principles of learning theory are applicable in many areas of human function in addition to their use in the mental health field. Psychologists are employed in industry and commerce, a major part of their role being that of providing advice on how the many human problems that arise among employees may best be dealt with or, better, avoided. The working conditions in many industrial enterprises are far from optimal. By studying these, and assisting in the development of working environments which promote the efficent functioning of the personnel concerned, the behaviourist can promote greater efficiency, and help reduce the incidence of mental health problems among workers. As industrial competition intensifies, this application of learning theory is likely to receive increasing emphasis.

In conclusion, we have to say that Paul's (1967) quintessential question – 'What treatment by *whom* is most effective for *this* individual with *that* specific problem and under *which* set of circumstances'? – remains unanswered. What is clear is that behavioural approaches are *the* treatment for *some* problems affecting *many* individuals at *certain* times, and that they can contribute usefully in many other situations.

The scientific rigour brought to the field by behaviour therapists is helping to answer Paul's all-important question and to define more precisely the roles of behavioural treatments generally.

References

Abrams , D.B. & Wilson, G.T. (1979) 'Effects of alcohol on social anxiety in women: cognitive versus psychological processes.' *Journal of Abnormal Psychology*, **88**, 161–73.

Achenbach, T.M. & Edelbrock, C.S. (1979) 'The child behaviour profile II: boys aged twelve to sixteen and girls aged six to eleven and twelve to sixteen.' *Journal of Consulting and Clinical Psychology*, **47**, 223–33.

Achenbach, T. & Edelbrock, C.S. (1983) *Manual for the Child Behaviour Checklist and Revised Child Behaviour Profile*. Burlington: University Associations in Psychiatry.

Agras, W.S. (1984) 'The behavioural treatment of somatic disorders.' In Gentry, W.D. (Ed.) *Handbook of Behavioural Medicine*. New York: Guilford.

Alberti, R.E & Emmons, M.L. (1974) *Your Perfect Right: A Guide to Assertive Behaviour*. San Luis Opispo: Impact Publishers.

Allen, G. (1976) 'Twin studies of affective illness.' *Archives of General Psychiatry*, **33**, 1476–8.

American Psychiatric Association (1987) *Diagnostic and Statistical Manual* (3rd ed – revised). Washington, D.C.: A.P.A.

Annon, J.S. (1975) *The Behavioural Treatment of Sexual Problems, Vol. 2: Intensive Therapy*. Honolulu: Enabling Systems.

Arias, I. & O'Leary, K.D. (1988) 'Cognitive-behavioural treatment of physical aggression in marriage.' In Epstein, N., Schlesinger, S.E. & Dryden, W. (Eds) *Cognitive-Behavioural Therapy with Families*. New York: Brunner/Mazel.

Asher, S.R. & Wheeler, V. (1985) 'Children's loneliness: a comparison of rejected and neglected peer status.' *Journal of Consulting and Clinical Psychology*, **53**, 500–5.

Axelrod, S. (1987) 'Doing it without arrows' (A review of Donellan's *Alternatives to Punishment – Solving Problems with Non-Aversive Strategies*). *The Behaviour Therapist*, **10**, 243–51.

Azaroff, B.S. & Reese, E.P. (1982) *Applying Behavioural Analysis*. New York: Holt, Rinehart & Winston.

Bandura, A. (1969) *Principles of Behaviour Modification*. New York: Holt, Rinehart & Winston.

Bandura, A. & Walters, R.H. (1963) *Social Learning and Personality Development*. New York: Holt, Rinehart & Winston.

Barker, P. (1986) *Basic Family Therapy* 2nd. ed. Oxford: Blackwell; New York: Oxford.

Barker, P. (1988) *Basic Child Psychiatry* 5th ed. Oxford: Blackwell; Chicago: Year Book.

Barker, P. (1990) *Clinical Interviews with Children and Adolescents.* New York, Norton.

Barkley, R.A. (1989) 'Attention deficit-hyperactivity disorder.' In Mash, E.J. & Barkley, R.A. *Treatment of Childhood Disorders.* New York: Guilford.

Barlow, D.H. & Abel, G.G (1981) 'Recent developments in assessment and treatment of paraphilias and gender-identity disorders.' In Craighead, W.E., Kazdin, A.E. & Mahoney, A.E. (Eds.) *Behaviour Modification: Principles, Issues and Applications* 2nd ed. Boston: Houghton Mifflin.

Barrios, B.A. & O'Dell, S.L. (1989) 'Fears and anxieties.' In Mash, E.J. & Barkley, R.A. (Eds) *Treatment of Childhood Disorders.* New York: Guilford.

Beck, A.T. (1976) *Cognitive Therapy and the Emotional Disorders.* New York: Meridian.

Beck, A.T. (1987) 'Cognitive therapy.' In Zeig, J.K. (Ed) *The Evolution of Psychotherapy.* New York: Brunner/Mazel.

Beck, A.T. & Emery, G. (1985) *Anxiety Disorders and Phobias: A Cognitive Perspective.* New York: Basic Books.

Beck, A.T., Rush, A.J., Shaw, B.F. & Emery, G. (1979) *Cognitive Therapy of Depression.* New York: Guilford.

Bedrosian, R.C. (1988) 'Treating depression and suicidal wishes within the family context.' In Epstein, N., Schlesinger, S.E. & Dryden, W. *Cognitive-Behavioural Therapy with Families.* New York: Brunner/Mazel.

Bernstein, D.A. (1981) 'Anxiety management.' In Craighead, W.E., Kasdin, A.E. & Mahoney, M.J. (Eds) *Behaviour Modification: Principles, Issues and Applications.* Boston: Houghton-Mifflin.

Bernstein, G.S. (1989) 'Social validity and the debate over use of aversive/intrusive procedures.' *The Behaviour Therapist,* **12,** 123–5.

Birk, L., Miller, E. & Cohler, B. (1970) 'Group psychotherapy for homosexual men by male-female co-therapists.' *Acta Psychiatrica Scandinavica,* Supplement 218, 9–36.

Blanchard, E.B., Martin. J.E. & Dubbert, P.M. (1988) *Non-Drug Treatment for Essential Hypertension.* New York: Pergamon.

Blanchard, E.B., Schwartz, S.P. & Neff, D.F. (1988) 'Two year follow-up of behavioural treatment of irritable bowel syndrome.' *Behaviour Therapy,* **19,** 67–74.

Bornstein, P.H. & Bornstein, M.T. (1986) *Marital Therapy: A Behavioural-Communications Approach.* New York: Pergamon.

Braswell, L. & Kendall, P.C. (1988) 'Cognitive behavioural methods with children.' In Dobson, K. (Ed) *Handbook of Cognitive-Behavioural Therapies.* New York: Guilford.

Brena, S.F. & Chapman, S.L. (1983) *Management of Patients with Chronic Pain.* Jamaica, N.Y: Spectrum.

Cautella, J.R. & Wisocki, P.A. (1969) 'The use of male and female therapists in the treatment of homosexual behaviour.' In Rubin, R. & Franks, C. (Eds) *Advances in Behaviour Therapy, 1968.* New York: Academic Press.

Cattell, R.B. & Scheier, I.H. (1961) *The Meaning and Measurement of Neuroticism and Anxiety.* New York: Ronald.

Chess, S. & Thomas, A. (1984) *Origins and Evolution of Behaviour Disorders from Infancy to Early Adult Life.* New York: Brummer/Mazel.

Chomsky, N. (1964) 'A review of B.F. Skinner's "Verbal Behaviour".' In Fodor, J.A. & Katz, J.J. (Eds) *The Structure of Language Readings in the Philosophy of Language* (pages 547–78) Englewood Cliffs, N.J: Prentice-Hall.

Cicchetti, D. (1984) 'The emergence of developmental psychopathology.' *Child Development*, **55**, 1–7.

Coie, J.D. & Dodge, K.A. (1983) 'Continuity of children's social status: a five year longitudinal study.' *Merrill Palmer Quarterly*, **29**, 261–82.

Corcoran, K. & Fisher, J. (1987) *Measures for Clinical Practice: A Sourcebook.* New York: Free Press.

Craighead, W.E, Kazdin, A.E. & Mahoney, M.J. (1981) *Behaviour Modification: Principles, Issues and Applications* 2nd ed. Boston: Houghton Mifflin Company.

Crnic, K.A. & Reid, M. (1989) 'Mental retardation.' In Mash, E.J. & Barkley, R.A. (Eds) *Treatment of Childhood Disorders*, New York: Guilford.

Delora, J.S. & Warren, C.A.B. (1977) *Understanding Sexual Interaction.* Boston: Houghton Mifflin.

Derogatis, L.R. (1986) 'Psychology in cancer medicine: a perspective and overview.' *Journal of Consulting and Clinical Psychology*, **54**, 632–8.

DiGuiseppe, R. (1988) 'A cognitive behavioural approach to the treatment of conduct disorder children and adolescents.' In Epstein, N., Schlesinger, S.E. & Dryden, W. (Eds) *Cognitive Behavioural Therapy with Families.* New York: Brunner/Mazel.

Dobson, K.S. (Ed) (1988) *Handbook of Cognitive-Behavioural Therapies.* New York: Guilford.

Dodge, K.A. (1989) 'Problems in social relationships.' In Mash, E.J. & Barkley, R.A. *Treatment of Childhood Disorders*. New York: Guilford.

D'Zurilla, T.J. (1988) 'Problem solving therapies.' In Dobson, K.S. (Ed) *Handbook of Congitive-Behavioural Therapies*. New York: Guilford.

Edwards, N.B. (1972) 'Case conference: assertiveness training in a case of homosexual paedophilia.' *Journal of Behaviour Therapy and Experimental Psychiatry*, **3**, 55–63.

Ellis, A. (1958) 'Rational Psychotherapy.' *Journal of General Psychology*, **59**, 35–49.

Ellis, A. (1962) *Reason and Emotion in Psychotherapy*. Secaucus, N.J: Lyle Stuart.

Ellis, A. & Harper, R. (1975) *A New Guide to Rational Living*. Hollywood, CA: Wilshire Book Co.

Epstein, N., Schlesinger, S.E. & Dryden, W. (Eds) (1988) *Cognitive Behavioural Therapy with Families*. New York: Brunner/Mazel.

Eysenck, H.J. (1957) *The Dynamics of Anxiety and Hysteria*. London: Routledge & Kegan Paul.

Eysenck, H.J. (1960) *Behaviour Therapy and the Neuroses*. New York: Pergamon.

Farquhar, J.W., Maccoby, N. & Solomon, D.S. (1984) 'Community applications of behavioural medicine.' In Gentry, W.D. (Ed) *Handbook of Behavioural Medicine*. New York: Guilford.

Fensterheim, H. & Baer, J. (1975) *Don't Say Yes When You Want to Say No*. New York: Dell.

Fensterheim, H. & Glazer, H.I. (1983) *Behavioural Psychotherapy*. New York: Brunner/Mazel.

Feuerstein, M. Labbe, E.E. & Kuczierczyk, A.J. (1986) *Health Psychology: A Psychobiological Perspective*. New York: Plenum.

Foster, S.L. & Robin, A.L. (1989) 'Parent Adolescent Conflict.' In Mash, E.J. & Barkley, R.A. (Eds) *Treatment of Childhood Disorders*. New York: Guilford.

Gardner, B.T. & Gardner, R.A. (1975) 'Evidence for sentence constituents in the early utterances of child and chimpanzee.' *Journal of Experimental Psychology*, **104**, 244–67.

Gardner, H. (1985) *The Mind's New Science: A History of the Cognitive Revolution*. New York: Basic Books.

Gentry, W.D. (1984) *Handbook of Behavioural Medicine*. New York: Guilford.

Gentry, W.D. & Kobasa, S.C.O. (1984) 'Social and psychological resources mediating stress-illness relationships in humans.' In Gentry. W.D. (Ed) *Handbook of Behavioural Medicine*. New York: Guilford.

Goldstein, A.P., Heller, K. & Sechrest, L.B. (1966) *Psychotherapy and the Psychology of Behaviour Change.* New York: Wiley.

Goldfried, M.R. & Pomeran, D.M. (1968) 'Role of assessment in behaviour modification.' *Psychological Reports,* **23**, 75–8.

Graham, K,. (1980) 'Theories of intoxicated aggression.' *Canadian Journal of Behavioural Science,* **12**, 141–8.

Graham, K., LaRocque, L., Yetman, R., Ross, T.J. & Guistra, E. (1980) 'Aggression and barroom environments.' *Journal of Studies on Alcohol,* **41**, 277–92.

Griffith, R.G. & Spreat, S. (1989) 'Aversive behaviour modification procedures and the use of professional judgment.' *The Behaviour Therapist,* **112**, 143–6.

Guilford, J.P. (1977) *Way Beyond IQ: Guide to Improving Intelligence and Creativity.* Great Neck, NY: Creative Synergistic Associates.

Harris, S.L. (1989) 'Training parents of children with autism.' *The Behaviour Therapist,* **12**, 219–21.

Hebb, D.O. (1966) *Psychology.* Philadelphia: W.B. Saunders.

Herman, S.H., Barlow, D.H. & Agras, W.S. (1974) 'An experimental analysis of exposure to "explicit" heterosexual stimuli as an effective variable in changing arousal patterns of homosexuals.' *Behaviour Research and Therapy,* **12**, 335–45.

Hersen, M. & Barlow, D.H. (1976) *Single Case Experimental Design: Strategies for Studying Behaviour Change.* New York: Pergamon.

Hersen, M. & Bellack, A.S. (1981) 'Treatment of chronic mental patients.' In Craighead, W.E. & Mahoney, M.J. (Eds) *Behaviour Modification: Principles, Issues and Applications* 2nd ed. Boston: Houghton Mifflin Co.

Himelein, M. (1989) 'Victims of burglary: a cognitive analysis of psychological responses.' *The Behaviour Therapist,* **12**, 99–104.

Horton, A.M. (1988) 'The use of systematic desensitization with a brain injured male: A case report.' *The Behaviour Therapist,* **11** (1), 20–2.

Hulse, S.H., Deese, J. & Egeth, H. (1975) *The Psychology of Learning.* New York: McGraw-Hill.

Jacobsen, J.W. (1982) 'Problem behaviour and psychiatric impairment within a developmentally disabled population. I. Behaviour frequency.' *Applied Research in Mental Retardation,* **3**, 121–39.

Jacobson, N. (1977) 'Problem solving and contingency contracting in the treatment of marital discord.' *Journal of Consulting and Clinical Psychology,* **45**, 92–100.

Jacobson, N.S. & Dallas, M. (1981) 'Helping married couples improve their relationships.' In Craighead, W.E., Kazdin, A.E.

& Mahoney, M.J. (Eds) *Behaviour Modification: Principles, Issues and Applications* 2nd Ed. Boston: Houghton Mifflin Co.

Jacobson, N.S. & Margoun, G. (1979) *Marital Therapy: Strategies Based on Social Learning and Behaviour Exchange Principles.* New York: Brunner/Mazel.

Janis, J.L. (1984) 'The patient as decision maker.' In Gentry, W.D. (Ed) *Handbook of Behavioural Medicine.* New York: Guilford.

Jay, S.M., Elliott, C. & Varni, J.W. (1986) 'Acute and chronic pain in adults and children with cancer.' *Journal of Consulting and Clinical Psychology,* **54**, 601–7.

Kanfer, F.E. & Saslow, G. (1969) 'Behavioural diagnosis.' In Franks, C.M. (Ed) *Behaviour Therapy: Appraisal and Status.* New York: McGraw-Hill.

Kaplan, H.S. (1975) *The Illustrated Manual of Sex Therapy.* New York: A. and W. Visual Library.

Kaplan, S.J. (1986) *The Private Practice of Behaviour Therapy.* New York: Plenum Press.

Kazdin, A.E. (1985) *Treatment of Antisocial Behaviour in Children.* Homewood, Ill: Dorsey Press.

Kazdin, A.E. (1989) 'Childhood depression.' In Mash, E.T. & Barkley, R.A. *Treatment of Childhood Disorders.* New York: Guilford.

Kendall, P.C. & Braswell, L. (1985) *Cognitive-Behavioural Therapy for Impulsive Children.* New York: Guilford.

Kellerman, J. & Varni, J.W. (1982) 'Paediatric haematology.' In Russo, D.C. & Varni, J.W. (Eds) *Behavioural Paediatrics: Research and Practice.* New York: Plenum.

Kohler, W. (1925) *The Mentality of Apes.* New York: Harcourt Brace.

Lacks, P. (1987) *Behavioural Treatment for Persistent Insomnia.* New York: Pergamon.

Lang, A.R., Goeckner, D.J., Adesso, V.J. & Marlatt, G.A. (1975) 'Effects of alcohol on aggression in male social drinkers.' *Journal of Abnormal Psychology,* **84**, 508–18.

Lange, A.J. & Jakubowski, P. (1976) *Responsible Assertive Behaviour.* Champaign, Ill: Research Press.

LaVigna, G. & Donellan, A. (1986) *Alternatives to Punishment.* New York: Irvington.

Lazarus, A. (1984) *In the Mind's Eye.* New York: Guilford.

Leff, J.P. & Vaughn, C. (1985) *Expressed Emotion in Families.* New York: Guilford.

Leslie, L.A. & Epstein, N. (1988) 'Cognitive-behavioural treatment of remarried families.' In Epstein, N., Schlesinger, S.E. &

Dryden, W. *Cognitive Behavioural Therapy with Families*. New York: Brunner/Mazel.

Levanthal, E.A., Leventhal, H., Schacham, S. & Easterling, D.V. (1989) 'Active coping reduces reports of pain from childbirth.' *Journal of Consulting and Clinical Psychology*, **57**, 365–71.

Leventhal, H., Zimmerman, R. & Gutman, M. (1984) 'Compliance: a self regulation perspective.' In Gentry, W.D. (Ed) *Handbook of Behavioural Medicine*. New York: Guilford.

Lewinsohn, P.M. (1974) 'Clinical and theoretical aspects of depression.' In Calhoun, K.S., Adams, H.E. & Mitchell, K.M. (Eds) *Innovative Treatment Methods in Psychopathology*, New York: Wiley.

Lewis, F.D., Nelson, J, Nelson, C. & Reusnink, P. (1988) 'Effects of three feedback contingencies on the socially inappropriate talk of a brain injured adult.' *Behaviour Therapy*, **19**, 203–12.

Lovaas, O.I. (1967) 'A behaviour therapy approach to the treatment of childhood schizophrenia.' In Hill, J.P. (Ed) *Minnesota Symposia on Child Psychology, Vol. 1*. Minneapolis: University of Minnesota Press.

Luria, A. (1961) *The Role of Speech in the Regulation of Normal and Abnormal Behaviour*. New York: Liveright.

MacIntyre, A. (1966) *A Short History of Ethics*. New York: MacMillan.

Mahoney, M.J. (1974) *Cognition and Behaviour Modification*. Cambridge, Mass: Ballinger.

Mahoney, M.J. (1977) 'Personal science: a cognitive learning therapy.' In Ellis, A. & Grieger, R. (Eds) *Handbook of Rational Psychotherapy*. New York: Springer.

Mahoney, M.J., Kazdin, A.E. & Lesswing, W.J. (1974) 'Behaviour modification: delusion or deliverance?' In Franks, C.M. & Wilson, G.T. *Annual Review of Behaviour Therapy: Theory and Practice* (Volume 2) New York: Brunner/Mazel.

Marlatt, G.A. (1983) 'The controlled-drinking controversy: a commentary.' *American Psychologist*, **38**, 1097–110.

Marlatt, G.A. & Gordon, J.R. (1985) *Relapse Prevention: Maintenance Strategies in the Treatment of Addictive Disorders*. New York: Guilford.

Martin, G. & Pear, J. (1983) *Behaviour Modification: What It Is and How To Do It*. Englewood Cliffs, N.J: Prentice Hall.

Masek, B.J. & Jankel, W.R. (1982) 'Therapeutic adherence.' In Russo, D.C. & Varni, J.W. (Eds) *Behavioural Paediatrics: Research and Practice*. New York: Plenum.

Mash, E.J. (1987) 'Behavioural assessment of child and family disorders: contemporary approaches.' *Behavioural Assessment*, **9**, 202–5.

Mash, E.J. (1988) 'Behavioural assessment of child and family disturbance.' In Mash, E.J. & Terdal, L. (Eds) *Behavioural Assessment of Childhood Disorders*. New York: Guilford.

Mash, E.J. (1989) 'Treatment of child and family disturbance: a behavioural-systems perspective.' In Mash, E.J. & Barkley, R.A. (Eds) *Treatment of Childhood Disorders*. New York: Guilford.

Mash, E.J. & Barkley, R.A. (1989) *Treatment of Childhood Disorders*. New York: Guilford.

Mash, E.J. & Terdal, L.G. (Eds) (1981) *Behavioural Assessment of Childhood Disorders*. New York: Guilford.

Mash, E.J. & Terdal, L.G. (Eds) (1988) *Behavioural Assessment of Childhood Disorders* 2nd ed. New York: Guilford.

Masters, W.H. & Johnson, V.E. (1970) *Human Sexual Inadequacy*. Boston: Little, Brown.

Matson, J.L. (1989) *Treating Depression in Children and Adolescents*. New York: Pergamon.

McCrady, B.S. (1985) 'Alcoholism,' In Barlow, D.H. (Ed) *Clinical Handbook of Psychological Disorders: A Step-by-Step Treatment Manual*. New York: Guilford.

McFall, R.M. (1982) 'A review and reformulation of the concept of social skills.' *Behavioural Assessment*, **4**, 1–33.

McLean, P.D. (1981) 'Behavioural treatment of depression.' In Craighead, W.E., Kazdin, A.E. & Mahoney, M.J. (Eds) *Behaviour Modification: Principles, Issues and Applications*. Boston: Houghton Mifflin.

McMahon, R.J. (1987) 'Some current issues in the behavioural assessment of conduct disordered children.' *Behavioural Assessment*, **9**, 235–52.

McMahon, R.J. & Wells, K.C. (1989) 'Conduct disorder.' In Mash, E.J. & Barkley, R.A. *Treatment of Childhood Disorders*. New York: Guilford.

Meichenbaum, D. (1977) *Cognitive-Behaviour Modification: An Integrative Approach*. New York: Plenum.

Meichenbaum, D. (1985) *Stress Innoculation Training*. New York: Pergamon Press.

Melamed, B.G., Robbins, R.L. & Graves, S. (1982) 'Preparation for surgery and medical procedures.' In Russo, D.C., & Varni, J.W. (Eds) *Behavioural Paediatrics*. New York: Plenum.

Melzak, R. (1973) *The Puzzle of Pain*. Harmondsworth, England: Penguin.

Miller, G.A. (1956) 'The magical number seven plus or minus two:

some limits on our capacity for processing information.' *Psychological Review*, **63**, 81–97.

Miller, I.W., Norman, W.H., Keitner, G.I., Bishop, S.B. & Dow, M.G. (1989) 'Cognitive behavioural treatment of depressed inpatients.' *Behaviour Therapy*, **20**, 25–48.

Miller, N.E. (1969) 'Learning of visceral and glandular responses'. *Science*, **163**, 434–45.

Millon, T. (1986) 'Social learning models.' In Cooper, A., Frances, C.M. & Sacks, M. *Psychiatry (Volume 1): The Personality Disorders and Neuroses*. Philadelphia: Lippincott Company.

Millon, T. (1987) *Millon Clinical Multiaxial Inventory – II* (Manual). Minneapolis: National Computer Systems.

Mischel, W. (1971) *Introduction to Personality*. New York: Holt, Reinhart and Winston.

Mischel, W., Ebsen, E.B. & Zeiss, A. (1972) 'Cognitive and attentional mechanisms in delay of gratification.' *Journal of Personality and Social Psychology*, **21**, 204–18.

Morton, T.L., Twentyman, C.T. & Azar, S.T. (1988) 'Cognitive-behavioural assessment and treatment of child abuse.' In Epstein, N., Schlesinger, S.E. & Dryden, W. (Eds) *Cognitive Behavioural Therapy with Families*. New York: Brunner/Mazel

Murdoch, D.D. (1985) *Alcohol and Aggression in the Natural Setting: The Influence of Cognitive Factors, Beverage Type, Dose and Sex*. PhD Thesis, McGill University, Montreal, Quebec.

Murdoch, D. & Pihl, R.O. (1988) 'The influence of beverage type on aggression in males in the natural setting.' *Aggressive Behaviour*, **14**, 324–36.

Newsom, C. & Rincover, A. (1989) 'Autism.' In Mash, E.J. & Barkley, R.J. (Eds) *Treatment of Childhood Disorders*. New York: Guilford.

Parke, R.D. (1972) 'Some effects of punishment on children's behaviour.' In Hartup, W.W. *The Young Child*, Vol. 2. (pp. 264–283) Washington, DC: National Association for the Education of Young Children.

Patterson, C.H. (1986) *Theories of Counselling and Psychotherapy* 4th Ed. New York: Harper & Row.

Patterson, G.R. (1976) 'The aggressive child: victim and architect of a coercive system.' In Mash, E.J., Hamerlynch, L.A. & Handy, L.C. (Eds) *Behaviour Modification and Families*. New York: Brunner/Mazel.

Patterson, G.R. (1982) *Coercive Family Process*. Eugene, OR: Castalia.

Patterson, G.R. & Reid, J.B. (1970) 'Reciprocity and coercion: two facets of social systems.' In Neuringer, C. & Michael, J.L. *Behaviour Modification in Clinical Psychology*. New York: Appleton-Century-Crofts.

Paul, G.L. (1967) 'Strategy of outcome research in psychotherapy.' *Journal of Consulting Psychology*, **31**, 109–18.

Pavlov, I.P. (1927) *Conditioned Reflexes* (Translated by G.V. Anrep). London: Oxford.

Pihl, R.O. (1983) 'Alcohol and aggression: a psychological perspective.' In Gottheil, E. (Ed) *Alcohol, Drug Abuse and Aggression*. Springfield, Ill: Charles C. Thomas.

Plomin, R. (1989) 'Environment and genes: determinants of behaviour.' *American Psychologist*, **44**, 105–11.

Pope, A.W., McHale, S.M. & Craighead, W.E. (1988) *Self Esteem Enhancement with Children and Adolescents*. New York: Pergamon.

Qualls, S.H. (1988) 'Problems in families of older adults.' In Epstein, N., Schlesinger, S.E. & Dryden, W. (Eds) *Cognitive Behavioural Therapy with Families*. New York: Brunner/Mazel.

Reed, B.R. & LoPiccolo, J. (1981) 'Treatment of sexual dysfunction.' In Craighead, W.E., Kazdin, A.E. & Mahoney, M.J. (Eds) *Behaviour Modification: Principles, Issues and Applications*. Boston: Houghton Mifflin Co.

Reynolds, G.S. (1975) *A Primer of Operant Conditioning* (Revised Edition). Dallas, TX: Scott, Foresman and Co.

Rosenthal, T.L. & Rosenthal, R.H. (1985) 'Clinical stress management.' In Barlow, D.H. (Ed) *Clinical Handbook of Psychological Disorders*. New York: Guilford Press.

Rush, A.J., Beck, A.T., Kovacs, M. & Hollon, S. (1977) 'Comparitive efficacy of cognitive therapy and imipramine in the treatment of depressed outpatients.: *Cognitive Therapy and Research*, **1**, 1737.

Russo, D.C. & Varni, J.W. (1982) *Behavioural Paediatrics: Research and Practice*. New York: Plenum.

Runco, M.A. & Schreibman, L. (1988) 'Children's judgement of autism and social validation of behaviour therapy efficacy.' *Behaviour Therapy*, **19**, 565–76.

Schlesinger, S.E. (1988) 'Cognitive-behavioural approaches to family treatment of addictions.' In Epstein, N., Schlesinger, S.E. & Dryden, W. (Eds) *Cognitive-Behavioural Therapies with Families*. New York: Brunner/Mazel.

Schwartz, G.E. Weiss, S.M. (1978) *Proceedings of the Yale Conference on Behavioural Medicine*. US Department of Health, Education and Welfare, No. (NIH) 78–1424. Washington, DC: US Government Printing Office.

Segal, Z.V. & Shaw, B.F. (1988) 'Cognitive assessment: issues and methods.' In Dobson, K. (Ed) *Handbook of Cognitive Behavioural Therapies.* New York: Guilford.

Selye, H. (1974) *Stress without distress.* New York: Signet.

Shapiro, A.K. & Morris, L.A. (1978) 'Placebo effects in medical and psychological therapies.' In Garfield, S.L. & Bergin, A.E. *Handbook of Psychotherapy and Behaviour Change.* New York: Wiley.

Sisson, L.A. Van Hasselt, V.B., Hersen, M. & Aurand, J.C. (1988) 'Tripartite behavioural intervention to reduce stereotypic and disruptive behaviours in young multihandicapped children.' *Behaviour Therapy,* **19**, 503–26.

Skinner, B.F. (1953) *Science and Human Behaviour.* New York: Free Press.

Skinner, B.F. (1971) *Beyond Freedom and Dignity.* New York: Bantam.

Sobell, M.B. & Sobell, L.C. (1976) 'Second year treatment outcome of alcoholics treated by individualized behaviour therapy: results.' *Behaviour Research and Therapy,* **14**, 195–216.

Spielberger, C., Gorsuch, R. & Lushene, R. (1970) *The State Trait Anxiety Inventory (STAI) Test Manual.* Palo Alto, CA: Consulting Psychology Press.

Spielberger, C.D. (1973) *Manual for the State-Trait Anxiety Inventory for Children.* Palo Alto, CA: Consulting Psychology Press.

Steketee, G. & Foa, E.B. (1985) 'Obsessive-compulsive disorder.' In Barlow, D.H. *Clinical Handbook of Psychological Disorders.* New York: Guilford Press.

Stevenson, I. & Wolpe, J. (1986) 'Recovery from sexual deviations through overcoming nonsexual neurotic responses.' *American Journal of Psychiatry,* **116**, 737–42.

Vandenberg, S.G., Singer, S.M. & Pauls, D.L. (1986) *The Heredity of Behaviour Disorders in Adults and Children.* New York: Plenum.

Veronen, L.J. (1989) 'Family survivors of homicide victims: a behavioural analysis.' *The Behaviour Therapist,* **12**, 75–80.

Vygotsky, L. (1962) *Thought and Language.* New York: Wiley.

Wadden, T.A. & Stunkard, A.J. (1985) 'Social and psychological consequences of obesity.' *Annals of Internal Medicine,* **103**, 1062–7.

Walen, S.R. & Perlmutter, R. (1988) 'Cognitive-behavioural treatment of adult sexual dysfunctions from a family perspective.' In Epstein, N., Schlesinger, S.E. & Dryden, W. (Eds) *Cognitive Behavioural Therapy with Families.* New York: Brunner/Mazel

Wallace, C.J., Boone, S.E., Donahoe, C.P. & Foy, D.W. (1985)

'The chronically mentally disabled: independent living skills training.' In Barlow, D.H. *Clinical Handbook of Psychological Disorders*. New York: Guilford.

Watson, J.B. (1913) *Behaviourism*. Chicago: University of Chicago Press.

Watson, J.D. (1968) *The Double Helix*. New York: Atheneum Press.

Weiss, R.L. & Perry, B.A. (1979) *Assessment and Treatment of Marital Dysfunction*. Oregon: Oregon Marital Studies Program. (Available from Robert L. Weiss, Department of Psychology, University of Oregon, Eugene, Oregon 97403.)

Wilkening, H.E. (1973) *The Psychology Almanac*. Monterey, CA: Brooks/Cole Publishing Co.

Wolpe, J. (1958) *Psychotherapy By Reciprocal Inhibition*. Stanford, CA: Stanford University Press.

World Health Organization (1978) *Mental Disorders: Glossary and Guide to their Classification in Accordance with the Ninth Revision of the International Classification of Diseases*. Geneva: WHO.

Zeig, J.K. (Ed) (1987) *The Evolution of Psychotherapy*. New York: Brunner/Mazel.

Author Index

Subject Index

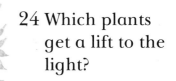

What is a plant?

Plants are living things. They come in all shapes and sizes, from tiny waterweeds to towering trees. Plants are different from animals in one very important way – they can make food for themselves from sunlight. Animals can't do this. They depend on plants for their food.

Where do plants grow?

There are about 380,000 different kinds of plants on Earth, and they grow just about everywhere – in fields and forests, deserts and mountains. Apart from air, the two things plants need are sunlight and water, so you won't find them in places that are completely dark or dry.

4

● All the food in the world starts with plants. You may eat eggs, meat and cheese but, without plants, no chicken or cow could produce these foods!

Are plants really alive?

Plants are just as alive as you are. They need air, food and water to grow, and they can make lots of new plants like themselves. This proves that they're alive. Things like stones and rocks don't feed, grow or have young because they're not alive.

● Corals and sea-anemones may look like plants, but they are imposters. In fact, they're animals!

Why do trees have leaves?

Like all plants, trees need their leaves to stay alive. Leaves are a tree's food factories. They contain a sticky green stuff called chlorophyll. The chlorophyll uses water, sunlight and carbon dioxide in the air to make a sugary food. The food is then carried to every part of the tree in a sweet and sticky juice called sap.

● If you've ever chewed a blade of grass, you'll know how sweet sap tastes. Hungry young caterpillars think so, too. That's why they eat leaves!

Why do some trees lose their leaves in autumn?

Big green leaves are useful in spring and summer. They make food while the sun shines and the days are long. When the days get shorter, there's less time for making food and the tree must live off its food reserves. Rather than feed their leaves too, some trees shed their leaves in autumn.

• The way plants make food in their leaves is called photosynthesis. During photosynthesis, plants take in carbon dioxide from the air. And they give out oxygen – the gas we all need to survive.

Why do leaves change colour in autumn?

• We call plants that lose their leaves in the autumn deciduous. Evergreens have tough leaves that can survive the winter. The trees still lose their leaves, but not all at the same time.

It's the chlorophyll in a plant's leaves that makes them look green. But in autumn, the chlorophyll breaks down. Once the green colouring has gone, the leaves' other colours show through – beautiful shades of red, yellow and gold.

Why do roots grow so long?

Long roots fix a plant firmly in the ground so that it won't fall over on windy days. But roots do another job, too. By spreading out far and wide, they can suck up water and goodness from all the soil around. Then the roots send the water up the stem or trunk and into the leaves.

● In the strongest winds, a tree can sometimes be blown right over. Its roots are wrenched out of the ground as the tree falls down with a crash.

● A wild fig tree in South Africa grew roots 120 metres down into the soil. If it was put on the roof of a 40-storey office block, its roots would reach down to the ground.

● At the ends of the roots are tiny hairs, which burrow into the spaces between the lumps of soil.

8

● Sunflowers not only grow up towards the light, but their flowers follow the Sun! As the Sun appears to move across the sky through the day, the flower-heads turn to face it.

Why are stems so straight?

A plant needs to hold its leaves up to the sunshine, which it uses to make its food. Many plants grow tall, straight stems, so that they can beat their neighbours to the sunlight.

● Not all plants have straight stems. Some have stems that bend and curl, clambering their way over nearby plants as they climb up to the light.

Which plants grow in water?

The giant water lily grows in the lakes and rivers of South America. Its roots lie deep in the mud and its huge leaves float on the water's surface. This is the best place for catching the sun! Each leaf curls up at the rim so that it can push other leaves aside.

● The giant water lily's leaves grow on long, strong stems. On the underside of each leaf is a web of supporting veins. This makes the leaves so strong that a toddler could sit on one without sinking!

Which are the smallest plants?

Although some types of algae grow to be the most enormous plants, there are other algae so small you can only see them through a microscope. The very smallest float in lakes and oceans, and are called phytoplankton. They're so tiny that whales catch millions in every gulp!

• The leaves and roots of water plants give food and shelter to many animals. But they're also places where hunters can hide.

Which forests grow in the sea?

Huge forests of kelp grow off the coast of California in the United States. Kelp is a kind of seaweed that grips on to rocks, and sends long ribbon-like stems up through the water. Some of the stems can be 200 metres long – as long as eight swimming pools laid end to end.

• Not all water plants are rooted in the mud. Some seaweeds float in the water, thanks to pockets of air in their leaves – rather like their very own rubber rings!

Which plant traps a treat?

When an insect lands on a Venus flytrap, it gets a nasty surprise! It only has to brush against one tiny hair on an open leaf tip, to make the leaf snap tightly shut. There's no escape for the poor insect. The flytrap changes it into a tasty soup, which it slowly soaks up.

FLY SOUP

● The bladderwort is an underwater meat-eater. Along its leaves are bubble-shaped bags, which suck in tiny creatures as they paddle past.

● Did you know that flytraps can count? The first time an insect touches a hair on one of the leaf tips, the trap stays open. But if it touches it a second time, the trap snaps shut!

one, two, three...

12

...fools a fly?

Pitcher plants have unusual vase-shaped leaves that tempt insects with a sugar-sweet smell. But the leaves are slippery traps. When a fly lands on them, it loses its footing, slips inside the 'vase', and drowns in a pool of juice.

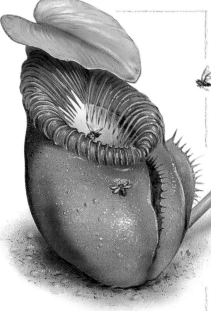

● Many meat-eating plants grow on wet, boggy ground where the soil is very poor. They need their juicy snacks for extra nourishment.

...snares a snack?

The sundew's leaves are covered in hairs, which sparkle with glue-like drops. When an insect lands on a leaf, it gets stuck fast. The more it struggles, the more it sticks. At last, the leaf folds over, traps the fly, and starts dissolving it into liquid food that it can drink up.

Why do plants have flowers?

Many plants have colourful, perfumed flowers that attract insects and other animals. The visitors feed on drops of sweet nectar inside the flower. As they feed, they pick up a fine yellow dust called pollen, which they carry to another flower. When the pollen rubs off on the second flower, that flower can start to make seeds.

● This plant is called hotlips – and no wonder! The lipstick-red markings on its leaves are a wonderful way to attract visitors to its tiny flower.

● Many trees and grasses spread their pollen on the wind. They don't need animal visitors, so they don't grow bright flowers.

● Pollinators, such as this bat, don't mean to get pollen all over themselves. But a cactus flower is shaped in such a way that the bat just can't help it!

Which flower fools a bee?

A bee orchid's flowers look and smell just like female bees. Male bees zoom to the flowers wanting to mate with them – but they've been tricked! The plant's just using them as postmen to deliver little packets of pollen to other orchids nearby.

● During the summer, the air can be so full of pollen that it makes many people sneeze. Poor things – they haven't got a cold, they've got hayfever.

Which is the smelliest flower?

The dead horse arum is well named – it stinks of rotten meat! But blowflies love it. These plump flies usually lay their eggs inside the rotting bodies of dead animals. They're fooled by the plant's rotten smell, and crawl inside it to lay their eggs, picking up pollen on the way.

Why is fruit so sweet and juicy?

Plants make sweet, juicy fruits so that animals will eat them. Inside every fruit is one or more seeds. When an animal swallows the fruit, it swallows the seeds as well. These pass through its body, and fall out in its droppings. In such good soil, the seeds soon start to grow into new plants!

● The cotton-top tamarin lives in the South American rainforest. It feeds mainly on fruit, especially delicious, juicy figs.

● You often see seeds floating through the air. Dandelion seeds grow their own fluffy parachutes. And sycamore seeds have wings, which spin them to the ground like tiny helicopters.

Which plant shoots from the hip?

The Mediterranean squirting cucumber has a special way of spreading its seeds. As the fruit grows, it fills with a slimy juice. Day by day, the fruit grows fuller and fuller until it bursts, flinging the seeds far out into the air.

16

Which seeds sail away?

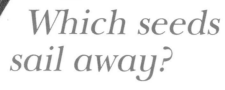

Coconut palms grow near the sea, so the ripe coconuts often fall into the water. Protected by their hard shell, they float out to sea. After several weeks or months, they are washed up on to a beach, where they sprout and start to grow.

● Fruits come in many different colours, but most animals seem to like red ones the best!

Which fruit gets forgotten?

Many animals feed on acorns, the fruits of the oak tree. Squirrels enjoy them so much that, every autumn, they bury some in the ground as a snack for when food is short in winter. The trouble is, the animals often forget where they've hidden their store, so when spring comes the young oaks start to grow.

When does a seed begin to grow?

Inside every seed is the tiny beginning of a new plant. This starts to grow when the soil around the seed is warm and damp. At first, the baby plant feeds on a store of food inside the seed. But as soon as its first leaves open, it begins to make food for itself.

● The seed of the horse-chestnut tree has a tough brown coat. This rots away in the winter, and the young plant bursts through in the spring.

1 The bean seed swells with water, and splits open. A root starts to grow.

2 Tiny hairs grow out from the branches of the root.

3 A shoot appears. It grows up towards the light.

Do all plants grow from seeds?

Strawberry plants don't need seeds to produce new plants. They can send out side shoots, called runners. Where these touch the ground, roots begin to grow, then leaves and stems. In just a few weeks, there's a brand new plant!

- The coco-de-mer palm tree grows the largest seeds. They weigh 20 kilograms – as much as a big bag of potatoes.

Which plant grows the fastest?

The bamboo plant is the fastest-growing plant in the world. Some kinds can grow nearly a metre a day. At that rate, they'd reach the roof of a two-storey house in a single week!

4 The shoot grows leaves. Now the new runner bean plant can make food for itself.

- A cycad tree in Mexico must hold the record as the world's slowest-growing plant. After 120 years, it was only 10 centimetres high!

Are fungi plants?

Fungi aren't really plants at all. They look like plants, and they grow in the same sort of places. But, unlike plants, they don't have leaves, stems or roots, and they don't make their food from sunlight. A fungus grows by soaking up food from dead animals and plants.

● Scientists have found over 100,000 different kinds of fungi – and there are probably many more. These tiny bright blue toadstools grow in New Zealand.

What puffs out of a puffball?

A puffball is a kind of fungus that looks like a large creamy ball. If you knock a ripe one, a cloud of dust puffs out of the top. This dust is really millions of tiny specks called spores. Spores do the same job as seeds. If they land in rich soil, they will grow into brand new puffballs.

- Did you know that the blue bits in some cheeses are a kind of fungus?

- There were plants on land long before there were animals. Some of the kinds that plant-eating dinosaurs ate are still around today.

Which are the oldest plants?

Soft mosses and tall ferns first appeared on land about 350 million years ago. But the very first plants appeared on Earth more than 3,000 million years earlier. They were tiny, microscopic plants called algae, which floated in the sea.

- One kind of fungus not only feeds on dead animals, it kills them first! The tiny spores grow inside live ants, feeding on the juicy bits of their bodies. Soon, nothing is left but the ant's dry skeleton, with the toadstools growing out of it.

Why do trees have thorns?

Trees such as the acacia have thorns to keep plant-eating animals away, but they don't always work. Goats, camels and giraffes, for example, have tough lips and mouths and long, curling tongues to get round the thorns. The plants will have to come up with another trick!

● The leaves on the lowest branches of a holly tree are the prickliest, to stop animals nibbling them. Higher up, the leaves are out of reach, so they're a lot less spiny.

Why do stinging nettles sting?

Stinging is another way plants protect themselves. Each leaf on a nettle is covered with little hairs as sharp as glass. If an animal sniffs one, the hair pricks the animal's nose and injects a drop of painful poison – ouch! It won't stick around to eat that leaf!

Which plants look like pebbles?

● Milkweed is a poisonous plant, but the caterpillars of the monarch butterfly eat it and come to no harm. It even makes them poisonous – so they don't get eaten by birds.

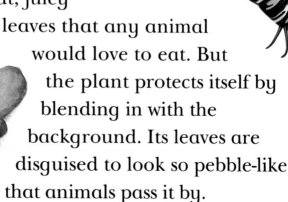

Pebble plants grow in the desert in southern Africa. They have two fat, juicy leaves that any animal would love to eat. But the plant protects itself by blending in with the background. Its leaves are disguised to look so pebble-like that animals pass it by.

Which plants get a lift to the light?

In rainforests the tallest trees spread out their branches in the sunshine, making it shady down below. Because of this, some smaller plants don't get enough light. A group of plants called epiphytes have solved the problem by perching high on the branches of trees and growing up there instead.

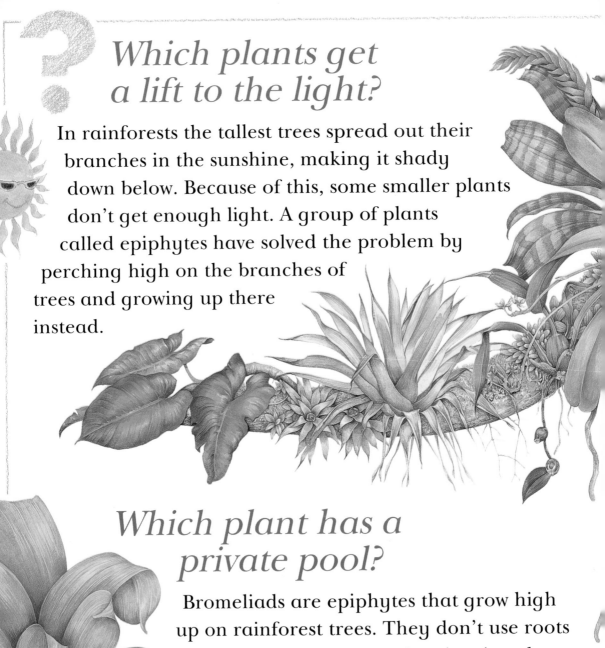

Which plant has a private pool?

Bromeliads are epiphytes that grow high up on rainforest trees. They don't use roots to collect water – every time it rains, the plants catch drops of water in a pool in the middle of their leaves. The tiny pools are perfect for tree frogs to relax in, too!

• It's so wet in a rainforest that many plants have leaves with downward-pointing tips. They're like drainpipes for the rain to run down.

• Lianas are climbing plants that dangle from rainforest trees. Some animals use them as ropes, and swing on them through the trees.

• Not all epiphytes collect water in their leaves. Some, such as orchids, have long trailing roots, which soak up water from the steamy air like a sponge.

Which plants strangle and squeeze?

The strangler fig is well-named because it strangles other trees to death! Its seed sprouts high up on the branch of a tree. Week by week, its roots grow longer – wrapping round the branches, down the trunk, and into the ground. The fig now sucks all the goodness out of the soil, starving its host until it dies.

Can plants grow in a desert?

Plants can grow in a desert, but they need special ways to survive. Cacti have spreading roots that slurp up any rain as soon as it falls. Then they take great care of the water, storing it inside their fat juicy stems. It may have to last them weeks, months or even years.

● Desert plants save lives! Many thirsty travellers have sucked life-saving water from the juicy flesh of a cactus.

Can you pick fruit in the desert?

Huge bunches of sweet, sticky dates dangle from palm trees, beside springs in the deserts of Africa and the Middle East. People have been picking the delicious fruit in these parts for more than 5,000 years.

• A gila woodpecker makes a cool nest for itself by carving out a hole in a cactus. When it leaves, there's a long queue of other birds who'd like to move in!

Can you find flowers in the desert?

Daisies, poppies and many other plants flower in the desert. The plants wither and die during the hot, dry months, but their seeds survive in the ground. When it rains, they soon spring into action. They grow into new plants and cover the dry desert with a beautiful carpet of flowers within a few weeks.

Which are the tastiest plants?

Spices are made from plants. They have such a strong smell and taste that we use them in cooking to give food a kick! After being harvested, most spices are dried, and then crushed to a powder that you can add to your food.

● Most spices come from plants which grow in tropical parts of the world. For hundreds of years, merchants have travelled around the world to buy spices at markets like this.

● Spices are made from different parts of plants. Pepper comes from berries, cinnamon from bark, and ginger from a root.

Why do carrot plants grow carrots?

A carrot is a tasty food – but it's not really meant for us! Carrot plants live for just two years. In the first year they make food, which they store in a fat orange root. They use up the food in the second year, while they're growing flowers and seeds – as long as the carrots haven't already been picked!

● Roots, berries, leaves and seeds – plants give us so many wonderful foods that some people eat no animal foods at all. They are called vegans.

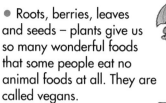

Do people ever eat grass?

Wheat, rice, corn, barley, oats and rye are just some of the grasses that people eat all over the world. We don't eat the leaves like cows and other animals do. We harvest the seeds. Then we either eat them whole, or grind them into flour to make pasta, bread and other important foods.

● Scientists can improve seeds so that they grow into stronger, healthier plants. This helps farmers to grow bigger and better crops.

What are old plants good for?

Three hundred million years ago, there were huge forests of trees and ferns. As the plants died, they fell into muddy swamps and were buried in the mud. Slowly, over millions of years, the plants were pressed down and turned into a black rock called coal. Coal is a fuel. We burn it in power stations to make electricity.

• The coal we burn today comes from plants that grew before there were even dinosaurs!

• Shampoos, perfumes, bath oils and creams are all made from sweet-smelling plants. That's how you smell so sweet!

• In some parts of the world, people run their cars on fuels made from corn, potato and sugarcane plants.

- The corks that seal bottles of wine are made from the bark of the cork oak tree.

- Many of the medicines we buy at the chemist's are made from plants.

What are plants good for today?

Today's plants are still giving us the food and oxygen we need to survive. They also help us to make lots of useful things, such as paper, clothes and medicines. Every year, scientists discover new plants, and new ways to use them. So let's protect our plants.

- All sorts of useful things are made from rubber. It comes from the sticky juices of the rubber tree.

Flax

Cotton

- Cotton cloth is made from the soft hairs that surround the cotton plant's seeds. Linen is made from the stems of the flax plant.

Index